Deliverance
from Darkness, Demons, & Disease

RODERICK AGUILLARD

Copyright © 2013 by Roderick Aguillard

All rights reserved. No part of this book may be used, reproduced, stored in a retrieval system, or transmitted in any form whatsoever — including electronic, photocopy, recording — without prior written permission from the author, except in the case of brief quotations embodied in critical articles or reviews.

All scripture quotations, unless otherwise indicated, are taken from the *Holy Bible, King James Version*. KJV. Public Domain.

Scripture quotations marked MSG are taken from The Message. Copyright © 1993, 1994, 1995, 1996, 2000, 2001, 2002, 2003 by Eugene H. Peterson. Used by permission of NavPress Publishing Group. Website.

Scripture quotations marked NLT are taken from the Holy Bible, New Living Translation, copyright © 1996, 2004, 2007. Used by permission of Tyndale House Publishers, Inc. Carol Stream, Illinois 60188. All rights reserved. Website.

FIRST EDITION

ISBN: 978-1-939748-40-9

Library of Congress Control Number: 2013922983

Published by

P.O. Box 2839, Apopka, FL 32704

Printed in the United States of America

Disclaimer: The views and opinions expressed in this book are solely those of the authors and other contributors. These views and opinions do not necessarily represent those of Certa Resources LLC, dba Certa Publishing.

Introduction

Across the body of Christ, most conservative leaders agree that America is in deep darkness. The kingdom of Satan has released major principalities over our nation to divide and destroy. *"The Lion is come up for his thicket, and the destroyer of the Gentiles is on his way. He is gone forth from his place to make thy land desolate; and thy cities laid in waste, without an inhabitant."* Jeremiah 4:7. Also, a host of demonic powers have arrayed against the church and the lost world to blind and to oppress.

Therefore, I believe this book was written for such a time as this. Pastors could use this writing as a deliverance handbook to set the captives free from demonic intrusion. So be it!

Rod Aguillard

CHAPTER ONE

Understanding the Nature of God's Kingdom

The Declaration of the Kingdom

I rejoice that in April 1968, I was translated from the kingdom of darkness into the kingdom of my heavenly Father's Son. In a moment of time without moral or merit, I was spiritually born into an eternal kingdom. Micah the prophet saw this King and kingdom coming, *"But thou, Bethlehem Ephratah, though thou be little among the thousands of Judah, yet out of thee shall he come forth unto me that is to be ruler in Israel; whose goings forth have been from of old, from everlasting"* Micah 5:2. The angel of the Lord made a declaration of this kingdom, *"to the shepherds in the fields at night and, lo, the angel of the Lord came upon them, and the glory of the Lord shone round about them: and they were sore afraid. And the angel said unto them, Fear not: for, behold, I bring you good tidings of great joy, which shall be to all people. For unto you is born this day in the city of David a Saviour, which is Christ the Lord."* Luke 2:11.

Jesus is the Christ, meaning He is the anointed one sent by our Father to establish His rule on planet earth and to destroy the works of the devil. Kingdom refers to the King's domain, implying the Lordship of Jesus over darkness, demons, and disease. Our Father has delegated this authority to His obedient church, to the going and giving church body. Therefore, as you and I surrender to His Lordship or rule, we have authority to deliver, to heal and to destroy all the works of the devil. Let's do it!

"Repentance is not complete until we see the King's domain and our dominion over demons and diseases." (Bill Johnson)

Yes, Lord. We see it; we seize it; we say it; and we do it in Jesus' name.

The message of the New Testament declared by our Lord Jesus is *"Repent for the kingdom of Heaven is at hand."* Matthew 4:17. *Repent* means that we "turn from the rule of sin, selfishness and Satan, and we turn to the rule of God and righteousness." Repent also means we make "an about-face and say *no* to the kingdoms of this world and we say *yes* to the kingdom and rule of our Father in Heaven." At our Lord's first coming, God's rule invaded planet earth. Everywhere Jesus walked, hell broke under His feet. The sick were healed, the lame walked, the demonized were delivered and the dead were raised. One more time Jesus!

In the fall of 2008, I was ministering at a church in

Bloomington, Indiana. During the night, I had a vision. Without any advertisement, men dressed in tuxedos and women dressed in elaborate evening gowns were filling up a stadium to meet a king. I stood in the midst of the stadium and realized the multitudes were coming to see a demonstration of God's authority and power. Then a voice came to me and assigned me to preach to this great multitude on this text, *"And, behold, I send the promise of my Father upon you: but tarry ye in the city of Jerusalem, until ye be endued with power from on high."* Luke 24:49.

In the dream, I had no Bible in my hand but as I looked down, I could see my oldest son running toward me to give me a Bible he had found. As I opened the Bible and was ready to declare God's Word, the vision ended. At that point, I was somewhat frustrated that the Holy Spirit didn't allow the vision to be completed with the thrill of preaching to such a great multitude of hungry hearts. Presently, the Holy Ghost is creating a hunger for God's Word and a demonstration of His rule and power over darkness, demons, and diseases. They are not coming to our fine buildings or even our sound doctrine. They are not coming to our Sunday schools or church picnics. They are coming to see the power of our Lord's kingdom. Join me. Let's move in it!

A Brief History of the Kingdom of God

In the beginning, God gave kingdom authority to Adam to rule planet earth. *"Be fruitful and multiply and replenish the earth, subdue it and have dominion."* Genesis 1:28 The first

Adam lost it. Satan usurped it through Adam's disobedience as recorded in Genesis 3:6. When man lost his rule and authority, he became a slave of sin, selfishness, sickness and the kingdom of darkness. Therefore, through Adam's sin, mankind lost kingdom authority and kingdom life.

The Good News: The Lord God didn't give up on the human race. Isaiah the prophet declared it. *"...when the enemy shall come in like a flood, the spirit of the Lord shall lift up a standard against him... and the deliverer shall come..."* Isaiah 59:19. At the cross, the deliverer/redeemer came and set us free from the rule and oppression of darkness, demons, and disease. The blood of Jesus redeemed us and set us free from the power of sin and sickness. Rejoice! He set us free from the curses of the broken law – poverty, sickness, disease, mental torment, and the second death. Indeed, our Father has given Jesus a name above every name! What the first Adam lost, the second Adam has regained. He is highly exalted! He is in supreme authority! He has delegated this authority to the body of obedient believers. See it...seize it...say it...and carry it out against demons, disease, and all the works of darkness.

The Nature of the Kingdom of God—The Four Expressions of the Kingdom of God

"For the kingdom of God is not meat and drink; but righteousness, and peace, and joy in the Holy Ghost." Romans 14:17.

1. **The kingdom of God is righteousness.** The Word of God declares that He, Jesus, was made sin with our

sinfulness that we would be made righteous with His righteousness. I rejoice in my state of righteousness. I rejoice in the power of the blood to keep on cleansing me from all unrighteousness. I John 1:9 declares, *"That if we confess our sins, He is faithful and just to cleanse us from all unrighteousness." Sin* means to "fall short of the glory of God." I still have issues with sin. Ask my wife; she knows me better than anyone. There are moments I am impatient with her. That's sin. There are times I am gruff in the tone of my voice when she misses the mark. That's sin on my part. There have been slips when I have taken a wrong look at the opposite sex. That falls short of the glory of God. The super-grace people don't believe in repentance or the confession of sin. But I do, and I am grateful that He instantly forgives me and cleanses me from all unrighteousness. Furthermore, by morning, the Holy Spirit leads me down paths of righteousness for His name's sake, the name of Jesus. Rejoice!

2. **The kingdom of God is peace**. *"Therefore being justified by faith (in the blood of Jesus) we have peace with God through our Lord Jesus Christ."* Romans 5:1. I rejoice that we serve the God of peace. I have peace with all men. Peace is power. The enemy of peace is distraction. As human beings, we are easily distracted and lose our peace. At home, during the college football season, I will watch and pull for the Louisiana State

University Tigers. When they playing badly, I lose my peace. In the past, I simply would turn off the TV and go outside and worship the God of creation. Football is not worth my peace. When someone offends me, I forgive. I simply let it go and keep my peace. No one's offense is worth me losing my peace. Peace is power!

3. **The kingdom of God is joy.** We serve the God of joy. *"In His presence there is fullness of joy…"* Psalms 16:11. Joy is the DNA of our heavenly Father: There is no sorrow in God…no anxiety in God. There is no sadness in God, just gladness and joy! Joy is not the absence of trials or problems. <u>Joy is the absence of defeat, despair, and depression.</u> <u>I have discovered that in much sorrow, there is joy.</u> There may be weeping for the night but joy comes in the morning. When our lovely Lynne (my oldest daughter) took her life at 44 years of age, marvelous Mary and I wept a river. But the comforter came. The Holy Spirit bandaged our wounds and released great joy within our hearts. We sorely miss her but we look forward with anticipation and joy that we will see her again in Heaven. The joy of the Lord has become our strength. As vessels of joy, we bring the kingdom of God to the body of Christ. As vessels of hope, we declare throughout our nation that a better day is coming. Let's rejoice in the great goodness of our Father!

4. **The kingdom of God is not in word but in power.**

"For the kingdom of God is not in word, but in power." I Corinthians 4:20. The kingdom of God is power to face the storms of life and to go through them. The kingdom of God is power to forgive all offenses and offenders. Yes it is! The kingdom of God is power to speak to your mountains and remove the resistance facing you. It is the power to overcome darkness and diseases, to love the unlovely, to bring Jesus to our generation. The kingdom of God is the power to stand against socialism, Islam, humanism, and the moral perversion of our nation; to engage the culture and take back our nation from the grip of principalities and powers. The kingdom of God is the power to reach the nations and win a world to Jesus; to heal and deliver the sick and the oppressed. *"...But if I with the finger of God cast out devils, no doubt the kingdom of God is come upon you!"* Luke 11:20. Once again, as it was written earlier, "Repentance is not complete until I see the King's domain and my dominion over demons and diseases." (Bill Johnson).

How to Experience or to Encounter the Kingdom of God

First of all, you must be born again, *"unless a man is born of water and the spirit, he cannot enter the kingdom of God...the dominion of King Jesus..."* John 3:5. In 1968, coming off an all-night drunk, I encountered divine authority. With no morals or merit, I came under the convicting power of the Holy Spirit. In the conviction, He gave me a clear choice between the kingdom of darkness and death, and the kingdom of light and life. He showed me the sins I cherished: the night clubs and drink, the party life, and the gambling habit. He gave me these as a reference point of repentance, repent ye, the kingdom of God is at hand. I hesitated because there is pleasure in sin but then comes the awful kick-back. My marriage and family were broken; my body was broken; and my finances were broken. I said to myself, "These sin pleasures are not worth it," and I cried out, "Lord, help me! Lord, Master, Ruler help me!" I was convicted of sin, and when I said yes to divine authority and the saving power of my Savior, I was born into the kingdom of life, love, and light!

How do you keep experiencing the kingdom of God? How do you keep moving in His purity and power? First of all, it's not for the lazy and the half-hearted. It is for the disciplined, for those who go on to know the Lord. *"The law and the prophets were until John: since that time the kingdom of God is preached, and every man presseth into it."* Luke 16:16. We must press into the kingdom. We must take up our cross of self-denial daily and follow Jesus. The kingdom of God does suffer violence. We live in enemy territory and there is much resistance because of the darkness and demons. We must take the kingdom by force. We must enforce the victory of Calvary, the blood for sin; the crucifixion for selfishness; the resurrection for the anointing; and the scourging for healing and health.

To keep experiencing and encountering the kingdom

of God, you must take time out with the Lord, morning by morning. Daily, you have to sit at the feet of Jesus and experience His presence and His grace for the day. If you have little or no communion with the Holy Spirit, you have no grace or kingdom authority to overcome the darkness and the demons. If you consistently stay around problems or keep your mind on negative circumstances, you have no power to overcome. *"I have written unto you, fathers, because ye have known him that is from the beginning. I have written unto you, young men, because ye are strong, and the word of God abideth in you, and ye have overcome the wicked one."* I John 2:14.

Hurricane Isaac caused Lake Ponchartrain to flood the community I live in. In the small town of LaPlace and Reserve, 10,000 homes were flooded and the five buildings of the church and school I founded were under water. In the midst of the devastation, I became part of the staff and assisted in the recovery and rebuilding. After three weeks, I was spiritually, emotionally, and physically exhausted. In this exhaustion, I was having serious health issues with high blood pressure. I had no rest in the mind and no rest in the body. As I lay on a couch in my secret place, I cried out and these words of life came to me: "If I live in the past, disappointment and grief will overwhelm me. If I try to live in the future, fear and anxiety will torment me. So today, let His grace and joy keep me. For this I know, God is with me and God is for me." Following that moment of waiting and communion, peace came back into my mind and strength into my spirit man and body. In brief, if you don't wait, you don't win. *"But they that wait upon the* L*ORD* *shall renew their strength; they shall mount up with wings as eagles; they shall run, and not be weary; and they shall walk, and not faint."* Isaiah 40:31. Let us rejoice, the kingdom of God has come and He dwells among us!

CHAPTER TWO

Understanding Satan's Nature and His Kingdom

To overcome our enemy or to be free from darkness and demons we must understand who our enemy is. We must understand his diabolic nature, that is to know how he moves against us to steal, kill, and destroy. First of all, Satan's kingdom was and is established in pride and rebellion. You can read the description of his angelic glory in Ezekiel 28:11-15. His diabolical nature and fall is described in the angelic King of Tyre.

Before his fall from the kingdom of God, the devil was called Lucifer, the son of the morning. He was described as Mr. Music. Tambourines and pipes were in him. He was a majestic created angel that was filled with musical ability to worship the Lord God. He was also called the anointed cherub. Cherub is a being of angelic order connected with vindicating the holiness of God over the prideful sin of man.

As recorded in Ezekiel 28:15-19, the Holy Spirit describes the fall of this majestic cherub from his glorious service to the Lord God. Lucifer got caught up in his own beauty and splendor. In the pride of his beauty and brightness, he became his own authority. In Lucifer's fall, understand the principle of authority: God's throne is established in authority! Jesus declared after His resurrection that *"...all authority is given unto me in Heaven and in earth."* Matthew 28:18. Our Father sent Jesus to redeem man, to set men free from the power of sin, Satan and selfishness. Also, He sent Jesus to reconcile men to God and to bring men under His rule or authority. Therefore, we declare by the power of the Holy Ghost that Jesus is Lord. When I was born again, I met authority! He is my Father, I am His adopted son. He is my Lord, I am His servant. He is my commander-in-chief, I am His solider. I am a man under authority; therefore I am a man of faith and favor. I have the authority and anointing to set captives free… to heal the sick and deliver the demonized in Jesus' name.

In Lucifer's fall, understand the principle of rebellion. *Rebellion* means to "rebel, to resist; being disobedient to the will of God Himself." Rebellion is the principle of self-exaltation. Listen to the voice of pride and self-exaltation in Isaiah 14:13, 14.

"I will ascent into Heaven." "I will raise my throne above the stars of God." "I will make my mantle myself like the Most High" or in common language, I rule…I will do what I want to do. I pastored a church in Reserve, Louisiana for thirty-seven years. How often have I seen believers walk away with their "I will's" – I will do what I want to do; I am hurt, I am offended…I will not forgive…I will leave.

The vision of the church leadership is too much; it's too hard…I will leave and go down the road. These are the "I wills" of rebellion. To stay free from the darkness and demons, to stay delivered…we must denounce self-rule, or self-will. Rather, we must follow Jesus as Lord and stay in a spirit of repentance, dependence and obedience. God pronounced judgment on Lucifer's rebellion. *"He was cast out of the mountain of God and was cast down to earth. How art thou fallen from heaven, O Lucifer, son of the morning! How art thou cut down to the ground, which didst weaken the nations!"* Isaiah 14:12. To stay free from darkness and demons and to free others, we must understand Satan's structure and strategy for ruling nations, communities and individuals. Read and study Ephesians 6:1-12 to see the four-fold listing of the dark kingdom. It is a diabolical structure of controlling regions and even nations.

First, there are principalities: rulers, strongmen or generals who rule over whole regions and nations. There are several principalities assigned to take over nations. We must allow the Holy Spirit to reveal them and the church lead by apostolic generals and prophets who will push back the darkness and diabolical rule. In regards to the USA, the Holy Spirit gave me the prophetic warning, *"The lion is come up from his thicket, and the destroyer of the Gentiles is on his way; he is gone forth from his place to make thy land desolate; and thy cities shall be laid waste, without an inhabitant."*

Jeremiah 4:7. In the land of the free and home of the brave, the lion has come out of his thicket to destroy our nation as we know it and to make our land desolate.

There are three major principalities over America:

1. **The Principality of Humanism:** This demonic mindset has taken over the media, our public education and the minds of most political leaders. Under the diabolical mindset of humanism, everything is relative, there are no moral absolutes. There is no need for the Ten Commandments. There is no judgment. There is no heaven and no hell. If it feels good, do it. Abortion is the moral choice of a would-be mother. Same-sex marriage is the moral choice of two males or two females coming together in matrimony. In this mindset, America is going over a moral cliff. We have lost the moral roots that made our nation great, and like the Roman Empire, we are rotting away and being destroyed on the inside.

2. **The Principality of Socialism:** This dark ruler has taken over our national and political leaders to divide and destroy America. Socialism is a demonic mindset, it is an Anti-Christ form of government that controls and strips a nation of its individual freedoms. Socialism promotes the redistribution of wealth, to steal from the work force to support those who will not work. Obamacare is a masterpiece of socialism; to have a government constructed health care system costing billions of taxpayer's dollars. Panels of government ruled

doctors are being setup to determine who will receive health care in critical cases, especially in regards to the elderly. Many of the leaders in the Democratic Party are socialists and have no regard for the Constitution or for the Judeo-Christian values that made our nation great. The lion has come out of the thicket!

Socialism is a principality that has come to make our land desolate. Socialism is the bedfellow of Communism and Fascism. It is an Anti-Christ form of government that controls, oppresses, and steals individual rights and freedoms. Nazism under Adolf Hitler was National Socialism. Under the tyranny of Hitler, this Anti-Christ mindset murdered over six million Jews and brought Germany into destruction. The Executive Branch and most of the Democrats in the Senate and House are under the dark mindset of this principality. We are in the midst of a demonic take-over of health care, public education, and the business sector including oppressive bank regulations. As a whole the Constitution and Bill of Rights are being ignored and dismantled. Executive orders are bypassing Congress and the Constitution. We are on the brink of tyranny and Anti-Christ take-over. The Lord God has empowered the body to bind the strongman or principality, engage the culture, and take back what the devil has stolen, which is our Christian heritage and righteousness. Let's do it!

3. **The Principality of Islam:** This has been assigned

to divide and destroy America. Islam is a violent warring principality that is moving through Muslims for national takeover. In the United States, the average Muslim family is having eight children per household. Figure out the math, in the next thirty years they could take over the gates of authority through population explosion. Wake-up church, the lion has come out of the thicket to make our land desolate.

There are other principalities that release a dark mindset over regions and cities. Years ago, I had a castle vision in the heavens. I walked into a castle that was over the gambling city of Las Vegas. As I walked in, I knew I was in a demonic stronghold. Men dressed like kings were in slow but deliberate moves operating over a black-jack table, a roulette table, slot machines, etc. I looked on the wall of the castle and there were large switch gear boxes. I knew what to do…from one switch box to the other, I threw the switches down into an off position and shut down each area of gambling one by one. Then in fear, I ran out of the castle. We have authority to bind the strongman over cities and regions thereby, shutting down the works of darkness giving us a power for a takeover and the harvest of souls. Let's do it!

The second listing of Satan's strategy for oppression and control is *powers*. *"We are against principalities and powers…"* Ephesians 6:12. Powers are demon spirits that are under the ruling principalities. They derive their power from and execute the will of the principalities or strongmen. There are many evil spirits that carry out Satan's plan of darkness and oppression over cities, communities or individuals. In regards to individuals, there is a spirit of depression and despair and a spirit of suicide that work together to kill or destroy.

"Put on the whole armor of God that you may be able to stand against the wiles or schemes of the devil." Ephesians 6:11. The scheme of an evil spirit is to make an inroad into the mind of an unaware believer. The strategy of demons and darkness is to hammer one thought until it penetrates and oppresses the mind. There are thoughts of failure, thoughts of rejection and self rejection, thoughts of sexual lust and guilt, spirits or thoughts of fear and failures. Evil spirits have a voice and they have access to our minds. My oldest daughter, Lynne Aguillard Venus came under a spirit of despair and deep depression. In this oppressive state-of-mind, a spirit of suicide came to her and convinced her mind that taking her life was the way out for peace. On December 11, 2008, she listened to the voice of suicide and ended her earthly life. Lynne was a causality of war. However, our Father in Heaven had the last word. Suicide said death but as she died, God said life! What the darkness and demons meant for our destruction, God has turned it for edification. In our setbacks and sorrow, the Holy Spirit has birthed a greater capacity to love, to help the suffering, and to deliver the captives.

In understanding the nature of God's Kingdom there are *"rulers of the darkness of this age..."* Ephesians 6:12. These are world rulers that deceive and control whole groups and nations through false religions. The spirit of Islam is a world ruler that is controlling the mindset of millions of Muslims. This Anti-Christ spirit has set a mindset of hatred and murder toward Jews, Christians, and the United States as an ally of Israel. The Muslim Brotherhood of Egypt is an enemy of Israel and believers of the Christian faith. Recently, the Obama administration awarded them two hundred Abram tanks and twenty F-16 Fighter Jets. This is an Anti-Christ, an Anti-American decision. During the summer of 2013, a Muslim Brotherhood individual, Muhammad Hosni Sayyid Mubarak, was removed as the president of Egypt by a military coup. In mid July of 2013, the Muslim Brotherhood, supported by the Obama administration began to murder Christians blaming them for the removal of their president. As I write this on July 16, 2013, the President of the United States nor any of his leaders is condemning this act of terrorism and murder. The liberal press is saying very little. It is an abomination to God and to the Christian heritage of our nation. God help us!

Then finally, in the nature or makeup of Satan's diabolic and dark kingdom there are "...*spiritual wickedness in high places*...." Ephesians 6:12. These wicked spirits are assigned to bring confusion to Christians. These evil powers wage their war against the local church. There is the spirit of witchcraft that wages war with curses, vexes, and physic prayers. I knew of a local church in Salem, Oregon that had a group of witches and warlocks that performed open warfare against them. It caused much confusion and division among the body and a major drop out of believers. The pastor finally found out the demonic source of bedlam when he discovered a group of these demonized foes lying out in a field nearby the church releasing their curses of confusion and division. He, along with his leaders, took authority and won the day.

Then there is the spirit of Absalom assigned against the local church in rebellion against the Father ministry. As a pastor, in the late 1980's or early 1990's, I experienced a major setback by a spirit of Absalom when spiritual sons turned against me. We eventually overcame this oppressive attack but we did have a fallout of membership.

Another wicked enemy assigned against the local church is the spirit of Jezebel. For a season, from about 2004-2008, I was helping a church in Tennessee with some senior oversight. During 2007-2008, I watched a Pearl Harbor attack upon that church body. A spirit of Jezebel manifested itself through a prophetic group of people and through certain uncovered women. The pastor failed to confront Jezebel by correcting the individuals that were slandering his ministry. Today, this 400 or 500 membership church no longer exists and following a foreclosure, the property and building is for sale. "God, help the pastors confront and cut off the ugly head of Jezebel when it begins to manifest through rebellious believers or demonic plants."

Understanding Satan's Diabolic Nature Through Names and Descriptions as Recorded in Scripture

Satan: *"And the Lord said, Simon, behold Satan hath desired to have you, that he may sift you as wheat."* (Luke

22:31). *Satan* means "adversary" or the "one who stands against the church or the individual believer." Note: There are only two recorded personal visitations of Satan himself in the earth. The first is in the deception of Adam. Genesis 3:1-7. The second appearance is in the attempted deception of Jesus Christ. Matthew 4:1-11; Luke 4:1-13.

The Devil: *"Then was Jesus lead of the Spirit into the wilderness to be tempted of the devil."* Matthew 4:1.

Beelzebub: *"...this fellow doth cast out devils, but Beelzebub is the price of devils."* Matthew 12:24. Beelzebub was the Philistine God of flies, the dung God or the Lord of the dunghill. This gives insight concerning his vile nature.

Belial: *"And what concord hath Christ with Belial."* II Corinthians 6:15. Belial: Equivalent of Hebrew, BELEYAHAL, which means without profit, worthlessness, wickedness.

Dragon: *"And the great dragon was cast out, that old serpent, called the Devil and Satan, which deceived the whole world..."* Revelations 12:9. Dragon is used thirteen times in the Book of Revelation to describe the wicked work of Satan.

Serpent: *"But I fear, lest by any means as the serpent beguiled Eve through his subtlety, so your minds should be corrupted from the simplicity that is in Christ."* II Corinthians 11:3. Satan is the deceiver of the whole world. His main attack and objective over individuals and nations is deception.

The Accuser of the Brethren: *"...now is come salvation and strength...for the accuser of the brethren is cast down..."* Revelation 12:10. Tormenting thoughts of condemnation and false gossip come from the wicked accuser.

The Tempter: *"And when the tempter came to Jesus..."* Matthew 4:3. Tempter (PEKRASMOS) – to test or tempt. The powers of darkness will tempt us to sin by appealing to the lust of the eye, the lust of the flesh, and the pride of life. They will also test or stand against our confession of faith in the promises of God.

The Wicked One: *"...He that is begotten of God keeping himself and that wicked one touched him not..."* I John 5:18. The whole world lies under the power of the wicked one.

The Murder: *"Ye are of your father the devil, and the lust of your father ye will do. He was a murderer from the beginning, and abode not in truth because there is no truth in him..."* John 8:44. He is the spirit behind the murder of unborn children. God help America!

Cunning: *"Lest Satan should get an advantage of us; for we are not ignorant of his devices."* II Corinthians 2:11.

A Thief: *"The thief cometh not but to steal, kill and destroy..."* John 10:10.

The King of Pride: Leviathan *"His scales are his pride...he beholdeth all high things; he is king over all the children of pride."* Job 41:15-34. God deliver us from stinking pride.

He is Fierce and Cruel: *"And lo, a spirit taketh him, and he suddenly cries out; and it teareth him that he foameth again, and bruising him hardly departs from him."* Luke 9:39. There is no mercy in the darkness of demons.

CHAPTER THREE

Understanding the Nature and Power of Demons

What is a demon? The Greek word for devil is Daimoneon which can be translated as demon. Demons are a host of fallen angels that fell from glory with Lucifer in his prideful rebellion.

Matthew 9:32-34, Matthew 25:41 and I Corinthians 11:9-10. Through these fallen angels, Satan is maintaining the power of sin and curses on the human race. The fundamental reason for the suffering of the human race is through the work of demon powers. As I visited India, I saw the poverty and suffering caused by demons and darkness because of their false religion and idolatry. Visiting Bombay on one particular mission trip, I saw the suffering of masses as they slept in the streets and lived in shacks among the garbage dumps. As I stood in my hotel room overlooking the starving and the suffering, the Holy Spirit spoke to me that He was not in my fancy hotel room, He was out in the streets where the darkness was doing its destructive work. Jesus came to set these captives free and invites us to join Him. One root meaning of demon is shadow. Satan sends evil spirits on people who bring shadows or darkness over the mind of unsaved men or immature believers.

Demons are disembodied spirits looking for a home. *"When the unclean spirit is gone out of a man, he walketh through dry places, seeking rest, and findeth none. Then he saith, I will return into my house from whence I came out; and when he is come, he findeth it empty, swept, and garnished. Then goeth he, and taketh with himself seven other spirits more wicked than himself, and they enter in and dwell there: and the last state of that man is worse than the first. Even so shall it be also unto this wicked generation."* Matthew 12:43-45. These disembodied wicked spirits desire to express personality through a human vessel. They express depraved passions. Recently, a man by the name of Ariel Castro was arrested for kidnapping and keeping three women as sex slaves in his home for ten years. He was demonized. He was full of depraved passions that raped, impregnated, and then caused one captive to have five abortions through starvation and hand beating her womb. Three victims of demons and darkness. The demons or evil spirits express Satan's characteristics of darkness and destruction.

Listed are a Few of Their Personality Expressions:

A Spirit of Fear: *"For God hath not given us the spirit* *of fear; but of power, and of love, and of a sound mind."* II Timothy 1:7.

A Spirit of Depression: *"To appoint unto them that mourn in Zion, to give unto them beauty for ashes, the oil of joy for mourning, the garment of praise for the spirit of heaviness; that they might be called trees of righteousness, the planting of the LORD, that he might be glorified."* Isaiah 61:3.

A Spirit of Bondage: *"For ye have not received the spirit of bondage again to fear; but ye have received the Spirit of adoption, whereby we cry, Abba, Father."* Romans 8:15.

A Spirit of Deception: *"Now the Spirit speaketh expressly, that in the latter times some shall depart from the faith, giving heed to seducing spirits, and doctrines of devils."* I Timothy 4:1.

Spirits of Infirmity: *"And, behold, there was a woman which had a spirit of infirmity eighteen years, and was bowed together, and could in no wise lift up herself. And when Jesus saw her, he called her to him, and said unto her, Woman, thou art loosed from thine infirmity. And he laid his hands on her: and immediately she was made straight, and glorified God."* Luke 13:11-16.

Spirits of Anger and Bitterness: *"But if ye have bitter envying and strife in your hearts, glory not, and lie not against the truth. This wisdom descendeth not from above, but is earthly, sensual, devilish. For where envying and strife is, there is confusion and every evil work."* James 3:14-16.

Spirits of Blindness: *"Then was brought unto him*

one possessed with a devil, blind, and dumb: and he healed him, insomuch that the blind and dumb both spake and saw." Matthew 12:22.

Demons or Evil Spirits are Intelligent and Have Knowledge: *"And there was in their synagogue a man with an unclean spirit; and he cried out, Saying, Let us alone; what have we to do with thee, thou Jesus of Nazareth? Art thou come to destroy us? I know thee who thou art, the Holy One of God."* Mark 1:23-24. Also, they have emotions. They tremble at the name of Jesus.

Spirits Have an Ability to Speak: *"And cried with a loud voice, and said, What have I to do with thee, Jesus, thou Son of the most high God? I adjure thee by God, that thou torment me not. For he said unto him, Come out of the man, thou unclean spirit. And he asked him, What is thy name? And he answered, saying, My name is Legion: for we are many."* Mark 5:7-9. Many years ago, I was called to the house of a church member who was in major marital conflict with his rebellious wife. She had locked herself in a room and as I knocked on the door and called out her name, a deep male-like demonic voice responded, "Leave me alone!" I was taken aback; it was my first time to hear the voice of a demon speaking through a human vessel. She was never delivered and eventually ran off with another man in an adulterous relationship.

Demon Powers have Doctrines: *"Now the Spirit speaketh expressly, that in the latter times some shall depart from the faith, giving heed to seducing spirits, and doctrines* *of devils."* I Timothy 4:1. I have seen families leave our local church because of a Jezebel spirit that infiltrated the body with doctrines of devils and deception.

Demon Powers Can Even Perform Miracles: The revelator saw them. Revelations 16:13-16. A close friend of mine, David Hogan, is an apostle to the unreached Indians of the bush country in Old Mexico. He has related stories of God performing many miracles under his hand and the hand of his pastors. Over two hundred people have been raised from the dead and thousands more have received miracles of divine healing and deliverance. At the same time he has witnessed the power of evil spirits to perform miracles. Once he confronted an apparent warlock who turned himself into a panther. There is an evil supernatural world that has the ability to do worthless miracles.

The Whole Fallen World is Under Demon Harassment.

Demon powers inflict the three basic curses of the broken law.

1. **The Curse of Sickness and Disease:** In many cases, evil spirits bring on the physical afflictions. *"How God anointed Jesus of Nazareth with the Holy Ghost and with power: who went about doing good, and healing all that were oppressed of the devil; for God was with him."* Acts 10:38.

2. **The Curse of Poverty:** I have visited nations that are

under this curse. Haiti and India are two of the poorest nations in the world. The multitudes worship other gods and come under the demonic onslaught of poverty, hunger, and sickness.

3. **The Third Curse of the Broken Law is Mental Torment or Mental Illness:** (II Timothy 1:7; Matthew 4:23-24; 17:14-21.) Mental torment can be transferred down through generational curses. Start my wife here… My wife's side of the family has a line of mental torment. She had a young aunt that committed suicide. She had an older uncle that committed suicide. Her grandmother went to bed depressed in her midlife staying in a depressed state until her death in her nineties. My wife's mother had several nervous breakdowns and died in a semi-depressed state. Our oldest daughter came under this generational curse at the age of twenty-two. The scripture states that, "a curse cannot come without cause." An unrepentive sin can be an open door to physical and mental generational curses. Lynne, my oldest daughter became embittered, through martial conflicts. In the midst of this, she came under severe mental torment. My associate pastor and wife took her into their home for deliverance and freedom. During this short time period, several of us went into prayer and fasting. During the fasting, I had a divine impression to tell her she had to repent of her bitterness and forgive her husband. She refused to listen and the bi-polar

curse began to have full effect. That same night, she tried to stab my associate with an ice pick. We had to put her under a doctor's care; eventually in a mental ward and twenty-two years later she tragically took her life while in a state of deep guilt and depression. My lovely Lynne was a casualty of war. Therefore, let us realize that the darkness and demons wage war against our mind, emotions and physical life to steal, kill, and destroy. Let's take heed to Holy Ghost instructions, *"...Be sober, be alert because your adversary the devil goes about seeking whom he may devour..."* I Peter 5:8.

Through my forty-five years of serving my Father in Heaven, I have learned to live in the fear of the Lord, to stay low, to be sweet and to live in a spirit of prayer and obedience. I have learned that the power of the blood will cleanse me from all sin. The power of the blood will protect my mind from all the fiery darts of the wicked one. By morning, I take the blood for my sin, the cross for my selfishness, the resurrection for my life and my anointing, and the scurging for my healing and health. I will have more to say about this in a later chapter.

Listed are the Activities of Demons as they Carry Out the Curses of the Broken Law on Mankind:

They deceive: *"Now the Spirit speaketh expressly, that in the latter times some shall depart from the faith, giving heed to seducing spirits, and doctrines of devils."* Timothy

4:1. Demons can deceive carnal or independent believers not rooted in the word of God. They have the power to mislead and deceive believers not under or submitted to proper pastoral authority.

They have the power to torment the mind. In the Bible, the maniac of Gadarenes who lived in the tombs was tormented. *"And they arrived at the country of the Gadarenes, which is over against Galilee. And when he went forth to land, there met him out of the city a certain man, which had devils long time, and ware no clothes, neither abode in any house, but in the tombs. When he saw Jesus, he cried out, and fell down before him, and with a loud voice said, What have I to do with thee, Jesus, thou Son of God most high? I beseech thee, torment me not."* Luke 8:26-28. Phobias, guilt and condemnation, deep depression and despair are all examples of mental torment. I was called to a home of a believer who had an employee that he led to the Lord. The young man had watched the movie, "Exorcist," and it apparently opened his mind to a tormenting evil spirit. As I sat with him and began to minister to him, suddenly, he bolted and ran his head through a glass window. We pulled him out of the broken window, cut up and bleeding. At a later date, we cast the demon out of him and he became a settled and stable believer, Glory to God!

Evil spirits have the power to defile the mind! Impure thoughts from a demon will come against the believer's mind to defile his thinking. Men, don't open your mind to impure thoughts by watching sex scenes or half-nude women. This an open door to defilement and guilt. Obey II Corinthians

10:5, *"Casting down imaginations, and every high thing that exalteth itself against the knowledge of God, and bringing into captivity every thought to the obedience of Christ."*

Evil spirits drive or compel: For example, religious spirits or a Jezebel spirit will drive people into some kind of hyper-spiritual action. I have seen a Jezebel spirit overtake an uncovered woman and it pushed her into doctrinal error. She became very divisive among church people. Compulsive eating, compulsive shopping, and compulsive gambling are examples of being driven by an evil spirit. Often, people under compulsive behavior need deliverance and extensive counseling to become free and to maintain their freedom. In the Bible, there was a young lady that was driven by a spirit of divination. *"And it came to pass, as we went to prayer, a certain damsel possessed with a spirit of divination met us, which brought her masters much gain by soothsaying: The same followed Paul and us, and cried, saying, These men are the servants of the most high God, which shew unto us the way of salvation. And this did she many days. But Paul, being grieved, turned and said to the spirit, I command thee in the name of Jesus Christ to come out of her. And he came out the same hour."* Acts 16:16-18.

Evil spirits have the power to enslave: *"For ye have not received the spirit of bondage again to fear; but ye have received the Spirit of adoption, whereby we cry, Abba, Father."* Romans 8:15. This scripture refers to a religious bondage or slavery. I have pastored believers who lived in fear regarding their salvation, struggling to be at peace or to have blessed assurance. They were fear driven and lived in a works salvation mentality. Rather than living in the rest of the river they tried to live in the merits of their works.

The good news is that in Christ Jesus we are overcomers. We may get knocked down but we are never knocked out. And by the grace of God we always get up before the count of ten. The Scripture declares our certain victory *"And they overcame him by the blood of the Lamb, and by the word of their testimony; and they loved not their lives unto the death."* Revelations 12:11. With this last thought, let's take our place as overcomers and move in kingdom dominion.

Chapter Four

Kingdom Dominion

Y ou have been created for dominion! *"And God said, Let us make man in our image, after our likeness: and let them have dominion over the fish of the sea, and over the fowl of the air, and over the cattle, and over all the earth, and over every creeping thing that creepeth upon the earth."* Genesis 1:26. Glory be to God that we were created in His image. God is a spirit. Man is a spirit who lives in a body and has a mind. Like our Creator, we have the ability to think, to will, to love, and to make moral decisions. We are not like animals; we are a free-will agent that has moral power to choose between right and wrong; to love God or not to love God; to obey Him or to refuse His Lordship and His Dominion.

Our Father said in the beginning, *"...let them have dominion."* Genesis 1:26. *Dominion* means to "rule, to tread under, to have authority over." It is God's ability to rule and reign in this life. It is a God-giving creative power to change this world from darkness to light; from evil to righteousness.

This is exciting good news!

I stated in an early chapter that kingdom means the Kings Domain. "Our repentance is not complete until we see our dominion over demons and diseases." (Bill Johnson) I am pressing into a baptism of grace to see my Lord's total defeat of darkness, demons, and disease. As I see it, I will seize it and take dominion to set captives free. I have a close pastor friend that was just stricken with a malignant brain tumor. The kind of cancer is Glioblastoma or GMB, the most aggressive malignant brain tumor in humans. The survival rate with treatment is one to two years. The facts tell us there is not much hope. But God, *"Our God is a God who delivers..."* Psalms 68:20. He delivers us from darkness, demons, and disease. *"...the sovereign Lord rescues or delivers us from death."* Psalms 68:20. Not only does He deliver us from despair and disease but He delivers us from death. We are not standing in a place of defeat but standing in a place of dominion. The prophet declared, *"Because you speak the word of God, behold, I will make my words in your mouth fire and they shall devour your wood."* Jeremiah 5:14. Your wood is your worries, your fears, your adversaries, diseases, and premature death. We are standing in the place of dominion and deliverance, our victory is certain. Rejoice!

The first Adam lost dominion through sin and disobedience. Adam and Eve ate the forbidden fruit and were banished from the garden and the tree of life. Genesis 3:6-7, 24. Therefore, when man lost fellowship with God in the cool of the garden, he lost kingdom dominion and he lost the victorious and abundant life. When the first Adam lost dominion, he came under the power of sin and shame, darkness and demons. Also, he came under the curses of sickness and disease, poverty, and mental torment. He lost the joy of God's presence, the peace and rest of the river. Also, he lost the grace and strength of his life. Then the curse of death passed on all men. I hate disease and death. Death is our Father's last enemy and will be swallowed up at the first resurrection even our Lord's second coming. Rejoice!

Therefore, God sent the second Adam to restore what the first Adam lost to darkness and demons.

Four Purposes of His First Coming

1. **He Came to Redeem Man:** *"In whom we have redemption through his blood, the forgiveness of sins, according to the riches of his grace."* Ephesians 1:7.

Redeem Man: He came to set men free from the power of sin and Satan; from the four curses of the broken law being sickness/disease, poverty, mental illness, and the second death.

2. **He Came to Restore Fellowship:** *"To wit God was in Christ, reconciling the world unto Himself."* II Corinthians 5:19. Therefore, in the cool of the morning we can sit still and have vertical communion and fellowship with our Father in Heaven through the presence and power of the Holy Spirit. What a privilege! What a joy!

3. **He Came to Destroy the Works of the Devil:** *"...For this purpose the Son of God was manifested, that he might destroy the works of the devil."* I John 3:8.

We have all authority over darkness, demons, and disease. Again, we must get still enough to see it, to seize it, to say it, and then move in it by faith action. Let's rejoice, what the first Adam lost, kingdom dominion, the second Adam restored. *"For as by one man's disobedience many were made sinners, so by the obedience of one shall many be made righteous."* Romans 5:19.

4. **He Came to Restore Dominion to the Redeemed:** *"Then he called his twelve disciples together, and gave them power and authority over all devils, and to cure diseases."* Luke 9:1. We have all authority over demons and disease: see it, seize it and release words of dominion.

I am going to list seven steps to dominion – how to master adverse circumstances or to be victorious over the darkness, demons and diseases. *Dominion* means to be "above it, to be the head and not the tail."

STEP ONE to dominion is to ***accept your position as a dominion creature.***

"Giving thanks unto the Father, which hath made us meet to be partakers of the inheritance of the saints in light." Colossians 1:12.

Jesus said, *"I saw Satan as lightning fall from Heaven... behold I give you authority over all the power of the enemy."* Luke 10:18-19. As His sons and daughters, we must see it or receive it by revelation knowledge. Again, our repentance is not complete until we see our dominion over darkness, demons, and disease. We see it, we say it, and we live it for our personal freedom and to set others free!

STEP TWO to dominion is to ***accept your position in the body of Christ.*** The word of God tells us that we are baptized into the body of Christ and though we are many members, we are one. I Corinthians 12:13-14. You and I belong to the greatest and most powerful organism in the world. Following my oldest daughter's tragic death at forty-four years of age, the body of Christ came alongside us, embraced us, loved us, slept in our home to comfort us, prayed and supported us for months. Today, we are still standing and serving because of the grace released into us through the body of Christ. It was a major part of our dominion and victory in a tragic death.

STEP THREE to dominion is to ***walk in obedience and allow the blood of Jesus to daily cleanse you.*** Sin consciousness will destroy your position and exercise of dominion. *"Behold, the LORD's hand is not shortened, that it cannot save; neither his ear heavy, that it cannot hear: But your iniquities have separated between you* *and your God, and your sins have hid his face from you, that he will not hear."* Isaiah 59:1-2.

By morning, I take my place of dominion by enforcing the victory of Calvary. I take the blood for my sin, *"If we confess our sins, he is faithful and just to forgive us our sins, and to cleanse us from all unrighteousness."* I John 1:9.

I take the cross for my selfishness and the resurrection for my life and anointing. *"Likewise reckon ye also yourselves to be dead indeed unto sin, but alive unto God through Jesus Christ our Lord."* Romans 6:11.

And finally, I take the scourging for my healing and health. *"But he was wounded for our transgressions, he was bruised for our iniquities: the chastisement of our peace was upon him; and with his stripes we are healed."* Isaiah 53:5.

STEP FOUR to dominion is to ***keep your mind stayed upon the Lord.*** If you look at the world and its bad news, you will get oppressed. If you look at yourself with all your flaws and faults, you will get depressed. Too many negative thoughts will put you in a mood of despair and discouragement. But if you look to Jesus, you will move into the river of rest and peace. Our Lord Jesus is our source and power of dominion. I rejoice in the anointed prayer of Ephesians 1:17-19, *"That the God of our Lord Jesus Christ, the Father of glory, may give unto you the* *spirit of wisdom and revelation in the knowledge of him: The eyes of your understanding being enlightened; that ye may know what is the hope of his calling, and what the riches of the glory of his inheritance in the saints. And what is the exceeding greatness of his power to us-ward who believe, according to the working of his mighty power."* So today, sit at the feet of Jesus and receive the spirit of wisdom and revelation of your great victory in our King and His Kingdom.

STEP FIVE to dominion is to ***daily depend on the Holy Spirit for the power of dominion***. Daily walk with Him, and daily commune with Him. Honor the ministry of the Holy Spirit. Our dominion and authority is based on revelation knowledge given by the Holy Spirit. *"Howbeit when he, the Spirit of truth, is come, he will guide you into all truth: for he shall not speak of himself; but whatsoever he shall hear, that shall he speak: and he will shew you things to come."* John 16:13. As we experience the revealed word it will release dominion. As we see it, we decree it. *"Thou shalt also decree a thing, and it shall be established unto thee: and the light shall shine upon thy ways."* Job 22:28**.** Through the power of proclamation we express our dominion rights. The word of God is clear: Jesus is our Savior/Healer. Surely, He bore our sicknesses and carried away our pains. Exodus 23:25 has been an anchor to keep my children healed and whole, *"And ye shall serve the*

LORD *your God, and he shall bless thy bread, and thy water; and I will take sickness away from the midst of thee."* I decreed it every time we had dinner at night. They were in their late teens before they ever saw the white coat of a doctor. Rejoice!

STEP SIX to dominion is to ***realize your daily warfare with an unseen foe***. *"For we wrestle not against flesh and blood, but against principalities, against powers, against the rulers of the darkness of this world, against spiritual wickedness in high places."* Ephesians 6:12. They are arrayed against us, waging war on all fronts. Too often, believers blame God for their setbacks and sorrows. God hates evil. In our Father there is no darkness, none at all. To resist and to overcome the darkness and demons, we must know and understand that God doesn't send evil. He doesn't send sickness and disease. He is not involved in stealing, killing or destroying. Rather, Jesus came to give life and to give it freely and abundantly. So we must exercise dominion over the darkness, demons, and disease. *"...In my name, cast out devils..."* Mark 16:17.

STEP SEVEN to dominion is to ***daily praise God for our victory over sin, Satan, and sickness.*** By morning, *"I will bless the* LORD *at all times: his praise shall continually be in my mouth."* Psalms 34:1. I have a growing list of blessings that I thank Him for. I also have a list of redemptive names to praise Him for whom

He is. If you know who He is, you know what He will do. I am enclosing that list of redemptive names as an aid to help you live as a dominion creature, that is, to see your authority and to exercise it over darkness, demons, and disease. So be it!

Nine Redemptive Names Of God

1. JEHOVAH – TSID-KENU: The Lord is our Righteousness. *"He that knew no sin was made sin for us, that we might be made the righteousness of God in Christ Jesus."* II Corinthians 5:21.

   He was made sin for our sinfulness to make us righteous with His righteousness.

   "Much more then, being now justified by his blood, we shall be saved from wrath through him." Romans 5:9. I am justified, just as if I never sinned, I am declared not guilty, righteous in His sight.

2. JEHOVAH – M'KADDESH: The Lord our Sanctification. He is the Lord Our Holiness!

   At the cross, He took our selfishness to give us His unselfishness…He took our pride, to give us His humility. He took our lust, to give us His love!

   "He suffered outside the gate that He might sanctify us through His blood..." Hebrews 13:12. He has sanctified us; He has and is separating us from all that is carnal, sensual, and secular. So be it!

3. JEHOVAH – RAPHA: The Lord our Healer: *"Surely, He has borne sickness and carried our pains with His scourging we are healed..."* Isaiah 53:4-5. He was made sick with our sickness that we might be made whole with His health and healing.

   This name was decreed by the Lord Himself, not by someone who gave it to Him. *"I am the Lord your Physician, or I am the Lord your Healer...."* Exodus 15:26.

   "And ye shall serve the LORD your God, and he shall bless thy bread, and thy water; and I will take sickness away from the midst of thee." Exodus 23:25.

4. JEHOVAH – SHALOM: The Lord our Peace: *"...the judgment of our peace was upon Him and with this scourging we are healed."* Isaiah 53:5. At the cross, He took our fears, worries, and anxieties that we might have His peace.

   "Be careful for nothing; but in everything by prayer and supplication with thanksgiving let your requests be made known unto God. And the peace of God, which passeth all understanding, shall keep your hearts and minds through Christ Jesus." Philippians 4:6.

   Note: Distractions and offenses are the enemies of your peace. Let no event, no person, no sin or temptation steal your peace with God.

5. JEHOVAH – JIREH: The Lord our Provider: *"For ye know the grace of our Lord Jesus Christ, that, though he was rich, yet for your sakes he became poor, that ye through his poverty might be rich."* II Corinthians 8:9.

He was made poor with our poverty that we might be made rich with His wealth.

"He who provides seed to the sower will multiply your seed sown…" II Corinthians 9:10.

If you will simply obey: Bring your tithes and offerings to your local storehouse (your local church). God will open the windows of Heaven; you won't have room to receive it. Malachi 3:10-12. It is a done deal: Obey the command and receive the promise of abundant provision.

6. JEHOVAH – SHAMMAH: The Lord who is There or the Lord our Favor. *"Yet it pleased the LORD to bruise him; he hath put him to grief: when thou shalt make his soul an offering for sin, he shall see his seed, he shall prolong his days, and the pleasure of the LORD shall prosper in his hand.*

Isaiah 53:10 At the cross, He took our wrath that we might have His favor.

"…it's God set time to favor Zion…" Psalms 102:13.

"In everything David did he had great success because the Lord was with Him." II Samuel 18:12-14.

~ 47 ~

"….whatsoever I set my hand to do I will prosper…"

7. JEHOVAH – ROI: He is the Lord our Shepherd. He guides us into all truth!

"The Lord is our Shepherd, we shall not want…" Psalms 23:1.

"He makes me to lie down in green pastures; He leads me by still waters." Psalms 23:2.

Yes, He feeds me and He gives me rest and refreshment.

Our Great Shepherd, Our Lord Jesus tenderly leads us, loves us, guides us and will keep us safe and secure in His arms.

8. JEHOVAH – SABAOTH: The Lord of Hosts, our Protector.

"The Lord will keep you from all evil; He will keep your life. The Lord will keep your going out and your coming in from this time forth and forever more." Psalms 121:7-8.

He protects me from evil accidents, evil diseases, evil temptations, evil men, evil torment, and evil storms.

9. JEHOVAH – NISSI: The Lord our Man of War. *"No weapon that is formed against thee shall prosper; and every tongue that shall rise against thee in judgment thou shalt condemn. This is the heritage of the servants*

of the Lord, *and their righteousness is of me, saith the* Lord.*"* Isaiah 54:17.

"He prepares me a table in the presence of my enemies." Psalms 23:5.

Therefore, I break every vex and hex and every word and curse spoken against my home and family, the ministry, and my local church.

CHAPTER FIVE

Minimizing Casualties

I am going to compare the task of the church to the Gulf War, 1990–1991, to the purposes in the kingdom of God. The Gulf War mandate was to liberate the people of Kuwait from enemy take over. Our mandate, the mandate of the local church, is to liberate all men everywhere. Jesus said to *"go ye into all the world and preach the good news..."* Matthew 28:18-19. The good news is that Jesus, the deliverer, has come to set men free from darkness, demons, and diseases.

The Gulf War's primary goal was to drive out an enemy in order to liberate. The Bible teaches us that whole regions are held captive by Satan's kingdom. *"The whole world lies under the power of the evil one."* I John 5:19. It is the warfare mandate to continually push back powers of darkness.

Another truth of the Gulf War is that the advance technology and weaponry used was a major factor in the allies' victory. Jesus said the gates of hell shall not prevail against us, Matthew 16:18. The gates of hell are where Satan's generals confer for strategy against the body of Christ, God's army. Our Lord Jesus, our commander-in-chief, assured us that we have advanced weaponry. He gave us the keys of the kingdom. We have all authority and spiritual weaponry to bind and to lose. He, our commander-in chief, said and is saying: *"Whatever you bind on or forbid on earth has already been bound or forbidden in Heaven and whatever you lose or permit on earth has already be loosed or permitted in Heaven."* Matthew 16:18-19. (Refer to the exchanges of the cross in Chapter Six) In other words, we have the authority and power to knock out our enemies control and communication centers.

The Gulf War strategy was to first implement air war to make the enemy ineffective. Our fighter jets hit the main communication and control centers, knocking out their radar, air force, and centers of supplies. In the end, Iraq had no fight to hold off the ground offensive. The church must first realize that she lives in a world at war and then implement air war to push back the darkness and demons, and make them ineffective over cities and whole regions, *"...how can anyone enter a strong man's house and carry off his possessions unless he first ties up the strong man? Then he can plunder his house."* Matthew 12:29. I am the senior overseer of the Network of Related Pastors (NRP), a coalition of about forty churches in about eighteen states. We are churches that are gaining the high ground, winning souls, and making disciples. Most of the NRP churches have set aside united prayer meetings to do air war; releasing God's power to push back the darkness of our enemy.

Finally, another primary goal of the Gulf War was to minimize casualties. We live in a world at war. As the church challenges the evil in our cities and nation, there will be counter attacks. Different team members of a local body at different times will come under the attack of the fiery missiles of the wicked one. From 1988-1992, I was part of a church movement that was protesting at the gates of hell, the abortion mills. Our purpose was to protect and liberate the unborn from the murdering knife of the abortionist. In our war for the innocent, we suffered casualties of war: attacks of sickness and disease, premature death, family setbacks, etc. We did our best through air war or a prayer movement to minimize casualties.

A *casualty* is defined a member of the armed forces who is lost to active service; killed, or wounded, captured or missing in action. Across the body, there are thousands missing in action. Tens of thousands used-to-be's: I used to tithe; I used to be faithful to the Sunday celebration service; I used to fast; I used to pray; I used to attend a life group; I used to share my faith in Jesus. Casualties of war, no longer on the front lines for Jesus.

Brother Johannes was a leader of the International Prayer Movement. He went to Russia from 1985-1986 to do major air war in binding the spirit of death. When he returned home, he encountered a counter attack from the powers of darkness and became a casualty of war. A sickness in his body developed into a heart disease. He was down and out of action for three years then experienced a divine healing.

During his down time he learned three important lessons of spiritual warfare:

1. **Never underestimate your enemy.** Darkness and demons have the power to tempt, to deceive, and to divide. They have the power to release formidable attacks on the mind and the physical body. The scripture admonishes us, *"Be sober, be vigilant; because your adversary the devil, as a roaring lion, walketh about, seeking whom he may devour: Whom resist steadfast in the faith, knowing that the same afflictions are accomplished in your brethren that are in the world."* I Peter 5:8-9.

2. As we do damage to the kingdom of darkness, **counter attacks are certain**. When I joined the rescue movement in 1988 in the war on abortion, we suffered casualties through demonic counter attacks. My mother-in-law went into a serious nervous breakdown. My oldest daughter had her first major bi-polar episode which eventually destroyed her physical life. My oldest son left his wife for a company secretary. A lady lawyer active in our war on abortion was murdered and thrown into a Louisiana bayou. An active pro-life pastor lost his wife to a brain tumor. Another active pro-life pastor had a sixteen-year-old son who had kidney failure. The list goes on and on in regards to darkness and demons inflicting division, disease, and even death.

3. **He was not walking in an adequate spiritual covering.**
Over my forty-four years of being in active service in God's kingdom, I have learned four parts of an adequate spiritual covering:

The first and foremost part of spiritual covering is having a devotional life.

"If ye abide in me, and my words abide in you, ye shall ask what ye will, and it shall be done unto you." John 15:7. A devotional life is an intimate time of fellowship with our Lord Jesus. It is not automatic, you must take time out to abide: To dwell in; to make your home in, to make Jesus the focal point of your life; your frame of reference in all decisions and actions.

One of my life messages is by morning to sit at the feet of Jesus. Listen to the words of the Lord Jesus in regards to Martha and Mary: *"And she had a sister called Mary, which also sat at Jesus' feet, and heard his word. And Jesus answered and said unto her, Martha, Martha, thou art careful and troubled about many things: But one thing is needful: and Mary hath chosen that good part, which shall not be taken away from her."* Luke 10:39, 41-42. He said, *"one thing is needful...,"* to sit at my feet and hear His word. My entire ministry is borne at the feet of Jesus at daybreak. *"...they that wait upon the LORD shall renew their strength; they shall mount up with wings as eagles; they shall run, and not be weary; and they shall walk, and not faint."* Isaiah 40:31. To wait means to tie the loose ends together. To wait means to be still and to see what the Lord is saying. As you wait, you will get renewed which means an exchange of your strength for His strength. As you wait, you will get refreshed from on High. The Lord declared this truth to His people, *"I will be like the dew to Israel..."* Hosea 14:5. Of course you know that dew is a source of refreshment and replenishment for plant life. Dew will not fall in the heat of the day nor while the wind is blowing, the air must be still. In the still of the night, the invisible particles form to replenish the earth. The scripture admonishes us to be still and know God. In the still of waiting on the Lord, we experience divine osmosis: absorption of His grace; His grace or strength to be a great dad or mother; grace to be an excellent employer or employee; grace to be a loving husband or a submissive wife. As we are still, we receive grace to see the will of our Father; grace to be His will and grace to do His will.

A second part of an adequate spiritual covering is to be connected to the body of Christ.

God breathes on those who are connected. On the day of Pentecost, one hundred and twenty believers were connected. They were of one mind, their eyes on Jesus to be clothed with power from on high. The book of Acts records their unity. *"when the day of Pentecost was fully come, they were all with one accord in one place. And suddenly there came a sound from heaven as of a rushing mighty wind, and it filled all the house where they were sitting."* Acts 2:1-2. Every crook and corner of the house was filled with His presence and power.

The hundred and twenty were filled with the Holy Spirit and turned the whole world upside down. I pastored a local church for thirty-seven years and I have many testimonies of a united body releasing God's power for healing, deliverance, and protection. In the late seventies, I was on a mission's trip to South India doing damage to the darkness and demons. During my stay, I came under a serious stomach attack. Flying home from Bombay, I was sick from torments of thoughts of fear and death. Before boarding the plane, I put out an S.O.S. to my home church and the warriors united for my healing and recovery. Somewhere between Bombay and Israel, I was instantly healed and delivered. I rejoice in my connection to the local body. *"Now I beseech you, brethren, for the Lord Jesus Christ's sake, and for the love of the Spirit, that ye strive together with me in your prayers to God for me."* Romans 15:30. The apostle Paul knew the prayer power of a local church covering and beseeched them for air war protection and deliverance.

The third part of a spiritual covering for strength, health, protection, and overcoming the darkness and demons is to be a man under authority.

Luke Chapter 7, is the story of the centurion who had a servant sick unto death, as he met Jesus he said, *"Just speak the word and my servant shall be healed."* Luke 7:7. He concluded that he was also a man set under authority and he would just say the word and those under him would obey. Jesus said, he had great faith. A key to great faith and overcoming darkness, demons, and disease is to be a believer under delegated authority. All of my pastoral ministry, I had three spiritual fathers over my life and ministry. They had the legal right to set me down if I became a ministry out of order. Also, they had the grace and wisdom to walk with me through the storms and setbacks of life. I am here today because of those three men. They watched over me, cared, and prayed for me. Throughout my local church ministry we were closely connected and had regular fellowship. Every individual and every pastor needs a pastor who cares for their soul.

The fourth part of a spiritual covering to overcome demons and darkness is to walk in the life of faith and obedience.

"Above all, taking the shield of faith, wherewith ye shall be able to quench all the fiery darts of the wicked." Ephesians 6:16. By morning I receive a Baptism of grace to love God with all my heart, soul, and body. At day break, I receive a Baptism of grace to see the great goodness of my Father in Heaven and to live in the fear of the Lord, that is, to hate sin and to love righteousness. By morning, I receive Baptism of grace to move in the healing and delivering power of Christ Jesus. By morning, I use the blood of my Lord Jesus to cleanse and to protect my mind from the negative thoughts of darkness and demons. *"...Casting down imaginations, and every high thing that exalteth itself against the knowledge of God, and bringing into captivity every thought to the obedience of Christ."* II Corinthians 10:5.

Join me! Let's not become a casualty of war. Let's war together to minimize the casualties in our local church.

CHAPTER SIX

The Scriptural Basis of Deliverance from Darkness, Demons, and Disease

The Scripture declares the deliverance of the redeemed. *"And the law is not of faith: but, The man that doeth them shall live in them. Christ hath redeemed us from the curse of the law, being made a curse for us: for it is written, Cursed is every one that hangeth on a tree: That the blessing of Abraham might come on the Gentiles through Jesus Christ; that we might receive the promise of the Spirit through faith."* Galatians 3:12-14. In the meaning of redeemed is the concept of deliverance. The same word is used for God's deliverance of the children of Isaac from the slavery of Egypt. God came down to deliver His people from the hand of Pharaoh, a type of Satan. He delivered them and brought them into the land of promise. In 1968, I was delivered from Egypt, the world system, and I was set free from the hand of Satan and his darkness. In a moment of time, I was born again into a land of my heavenly Father's promises, power, peace, and purpose.

In the Word, redeemed is the concept of ransom and deliverance from the power of sin. Jesus Christ is the atonement for our sin. Through His precious blood He atoned for our sin. He paid in full the sin of mankind. He paid the penalty of sin by His death on the cross. Let's rejoice, we have been bought with the precious blood of Christ Jesus. *"...For ye are bought with a price: therefore, glorify God in your body, and in your spirit, which are God's."* I Corinthians 6:20.

In the Word redeemed is the concept of deliverance from the curses of sin. Jesus bore the sufferings of the curse; He took Satan's blows for us. There are four basic curses of sin that Jesus has delivered us from: the curse of sickness and disease, the curse of poverty and lack, the curse of mental torment or mental illness, and the curse of the second death. Based on God's word, we need to claim and experience our full deliverance from these curses that are inflicted through demonic powers. See it, then seize it, and bring His delivering power to a lost and suffering world. We have been commissioned to do so, *"...And he said unto them, Go ye into all the world, and preach the gospel to every creature."* Mark 16:15. In 1968, I was called in a vision of the night. In my calling is a mantle or an anointing of a prophet. I am a seer. For over thirty years, I have been seeing God's judgment on America for the murder of innocent unborn children, moral perverseness, and the outright denial of our Christian heritage.

Also, in my mantle, I have seen a demonstration of God's power and deliverance. Several years ago, in Bloomington, Indiana, I had a vision of men dressed in tuxedos and women in evening gowns going to meet a king. I saw a stadium being filled with little or no advertisement. Tens of thousands people coming to see the delivering power of God.

Let's consider deliverance in the earthly ministry of our Lord Jesus. *"The spirit of the Lord is upon me because He has anointed me to preach the good news to the poor; he hath sent me to heal the brokenhearted, to preach deliverance to the captives, and recovering of sight to the blind, to set at liberty them that are bruised."* Luke 4:18. Christ Jesus came to destroy the works of the devil. Great light came to dispel the darkness and oppression of demons. *"...For this purpose the Son of God was manifested, that he might destroy the works of the devil."* I John 3:8. *Destroy* means to "undo, to release; to set free; to do away with." He came to destroy the power of sin and rebellion; the power of sickness and disease; the power of mental illness; the power of poverty; prostitution and pornography; the power of abortion and the lust of gambling. The list of the works of darkness fills the earth with suffering. When Jesus came, He confronted the darkness and demons. Mary Magdalene was delivered of seven devils. *"And certain women, which had been healed of evil spirits and infirmities, Mary called Magdalene, out of whom went seven devils."* Luke 8:2.

Here are some Bible facts about our Lord's deliverance power to set the captives free:

First of all, Jesus ministered deliverance and healing by the Word of God, *"When the evening was come, they brought unto him many that were possessed with devils: and he cast out the spirits with his word, and healed all that were sick: That it might be fulfilled which was spoken by Esaias the prophet, saying, Himself took our infirmities, and bare our sicknesses."* Matthew 8:16-17. I rejoice that Christ Jesus is our Healer and our Deliverer. In scripture, demons and diseases often seem to be closely connected. In 1974, as a Baptist, I began to preach Jesus as our Healer and Deliverer from the powers of darkness. Shortly afterwards, my family experienced a counter attack. My three small children were under a spirit of infirmity for weeks. My home looked like a mini-hospital. In the midst of this trial, the Holy Spirit quickened me to pray Exodus 23:25 at our nightly family dinners. *"And ye shall serve the LORD your God, and he shall bless thy bread, and thy water; and I will take sickness away from the midst of thee."* Exodus 23:25. A few weeks later I was impressed to look around and all of my children were healed and healthy. Until they were in their late teens, they never saw the white coat of a doctor. Indeed, Jesus is our Deliverer/Healer.

In deliverance, Jesus Christ cast out the evil spirits: *"And he healed many that were sick of divers diseases, and cast out many devils; and suffered not the devils to speak, because they knew him."* Mark 1:34. Our Lord commissioned and empowered the twelve to cast out devils and to heal the sick. *"And when he had called unto him his twelve disciples, he gave them power against unclean spirits, to cast them out, and to heal all manner of sickness and all manner of disease"* Matthew 10:1.

Over the forty-four plus years of my ministry, I believe the Holy Spirit has given me the understanding in being equipped to move in the ministry of deliverance from darkness, demons and disease.

I will briefly describe three insights that may help you to understand and move in this much needed ministry to reach a lost and suffering world and to set the captive free!

1. **Understand the Trichotomy of man in casting out evil spirits.** There are three factors in man's make-up. He is an eternal spirit. At the new birth, a man's spirit is reborn or regenerated by the power of the indwelling Holy Spirit. *"Unless a man is born of the spirit and water, he cannot see the kingdom of God or enter the kingdom of God!"* John 3:3.

   -A man is a spirit who has a mind. The mind consists of an intellect, emotions, and a will. The mind is not converted at the new birth. The mind must be delivered of strongholds or demonic oppressions, and then the mind must be renewed by the Word of God.

   -A man is a spirit who has a mind and lives in a physical body. Also, the body is not regenerated at the new birth. It is dead because of sin and the body will grow old and eventually die. Meanwhile, the Lord has provided divine healing and health for our bodies to serve Him and others in full strength all the days of our earthly life.

2. **Secondly, understand and know that the mind is the battlefield. Evil spirits have access to our minds.** *"But I fear, lest by any means, as the serpent beguiled Eve through his subtilty, so your minds should be corrupted from the simplicity that is in Christ."* II Corinthians 11:3. The spiritual world operates through the thought realm. Temptations and demonic oppression comes in thoughts. In the garden, the serpent beguiled Eve with deceptive thoughts concerning the integrity of God's word: *"God had said you will not eat of the tree in the midst of the garden or you shall surely die."* Genesis 3:1. In II Corinthians 10:35, The Holy Spirit commands us to tear down negative thoughts and take authority over strongholds of rejection; of lust and sexual guilt; of bitterness and failure. I have ministered to quite a few believers who had a stronghold of depression coupled with suicidal thoughts. Demonic strongholds torment, defied, drive, and enslave. Our Father's heart for us is deliverance and freedom from the darkness and demonic thoughts. I will in detail cover the protection and renewal of the mind in Chapter Twelve.

3. **There are six basic areas of deliverance**.
   - Deliverance from sickness and disease
   - Deliverance from rejection, a sense of being unwanted
   - Deliverance from the root of bitterness, *"Follow peace with all men, and holiness, without which*

no man shall see the Lord: Looking diligently lest any man fail of the grace of God; lest any root of bitterness springing up trouble you, and thereby many be defiled." Hebrews 12:14-15.

- Deliverance from sexual oppression and guilt
- Deliverance from generational curses and spoken curses
- Deliverance from occult involvement and the resulting demonic intrusion

Over the next few chapters, I will briefly cover deliverance and freedom from these areas of mental and physical affliction. The truth will set us free! Glory be to God!

CHAPTER SEVEN

Deliverance from Sickness and Disease

In the beginning God made man in His own image. Man was created to be a ruler or to have dominion. Genesis 1:28. We were not created to be under the rule of sin, Satan, and sickness. Sickness, sin, and death entered the human race by one man's disobedience. *"Wherefore, as by one man sin entered into the world, and death by sin; and so death passed upon all men, for that all have sinned."* Romans 5:12. Yes, death passed upon all men through sin. Sickness is limited death. Sickness is the devil's main method of inflicting premature death.

After Adam and Eve had sinned, they lost the glory of God on their life, they were uncovered and naked. Thus, they lost His rule and His anointing. They lost His authority and protection. This is referred to as "the fall of man." Death entered the world; sin, sickness, and Satan began their rule.

Therefore, in essence, sickness and disease belong to sin and rebellion. It doesn't belong to the church according to Isaiah 53:5: *"But he was wounded for our transgressions, he was bruised for our iniquities: the chastisement of our peace was upon him; and with his stripes we are healed."* By the redeeming power of Jesus Christ, we are restored in authority, righteousness, joy, and peace in the Holy Ghost; healing and health to glorify God in our physical bodies.

In the New Testament accounts sin and sickness are closely related:

A man who had an infirmity thirty-eight years was made whole. Jesus said, *"Sin no more, least a worst thing come upon thee."* John 5:14.

Jesus healed a man with a palsy, *"son, thy sins be forgiven thee."* Mark 2:5 & 9.

"...the prayer of faith shall save the sick and if any sins be committed they shall be forgiven." James 5:14-15.

Here is a great truth, sickness is not from Heaven. It is not our Father's will for you and me to stay under the power of sickness and disease. God is love and light. *"...God is light and in Him there is no darkness at all..."* I John 1:5. There is no sin or sickness in God. A believer is in union with the life of Jesus and that life in us is light and it develops men into His image and glory. There is no sickness, no, not any in His image and glory, *"Every good gift and every perfect gift is from above, and cometh down from the Father of lights, with whom is no variableness, neither shadow of turning."* James 1:17. There is no variableness in the Father of lights. God is consistent and He is the unchanging Savior. It is always His will for our best. Healing and health is His best and its part of our redemptive blessings. There is neither shadow of turning. There is no eclipse in God. The sun is at high noon. God is all light; there is no darkness, no sickness or disease in our heavenly Father. Rejoice!

Two erroneous teachings claiming that it is God who sends sickness:

First of all, God does not send sickness on some people. This false teaching declares that Paul's thorn in the flesh was sickness. *"And lest I should be exalted above measure through the abundance of the revelations, there was given to me a thorn in the flesh, the messenger of Satan to buffet me, lest I should be exalted above measure."* II Corinthians 12:7. God did permit a thorn in Paul's flesh. He did allow an evil spirit to stand against Paul's efforts for the gospel. But the thorn was never defined as sickness. In fact, Paul describes his thorn as the opposition and persecution stirred up by a messenger of Satan to hinder him in carrying out the Lord's work. II Corinthians 12:10.

Secondly God does not send sickness to chasten us, to be our cross. *"For whom the Lord loveth he chasteneth..."* Hebrews 12:6. It does not say, "For whom the Lord loveth He maketh sick..." The word *chasten* means "child train", "educate" or "teach". Believers need to be taught, reproved, and disciplined. Our Father in Heaven doesn't need sickness as a rod of correction.

Satan is the originator and the source of sickness and disease. Satan brought sickness on mankind through sin. And generally speaking, he keeps sickness on the human race. Scripture indicates that the life of sickness is carried out by demonic powers. Paul's judgment of sexual immorality reveals to work of the destroyer. *"To deliver such an one unto Satan for the destruction of the flesh, that the spirit may be saved in the day of the Lord Jesus."* I Corinthians 5:5. *The thief comes to steal, kill, and destroy.* John 10:10. The thief is our enemy; the devil and his demonic powers. He seeks to hinder us, hurt us, and devour us through the power of sin, sickness, disease, and mental torment. *"Understand that evil life is causing sickness and destruction in the human body."* (T.L. Osbourne, *Healing from Christ*) It is possible for open doors of sin or ignorance to allow a spirit of infirmity to afflict the human body.

I have shared the bad news, but now I will share the good news. Jesus Christ is our Savior, He is our sin offering. He made atonement for our sin. Through the blood of Jesus, God paid the debt of sin. In the atonement, our heavenly Father recovered all the blessings of life lost by the first Adam. God paid the penalty of sin and the negative effects of sin. Glory to God! The prophet Isaiah declared that God gave His son for the sin of all men everywhere! *"Yet it pleased the Lord to bruise him; he hath put him to grief: when thou shalt make his soul an offering for sin, he shall see his seed, he shall prolong his days, and the pleasure of the Lord shall prosper in his hand"* Isaiah 53:10.

Yes, Jesus Christ is the Savior for the whole world. He was our sin bearer. *"For he hath made him to be sin for us, who knew no sin; that we might be made the righteousness of God in him."* II Corinthians 5:21. He was made sin with our sinfulness that we might be made righteous with His righteousness. Through the blood of our Lord Jesus Christ we have been declared not guilty but righteous in His sight. Rejoice! I am walking it out through the continual cleansing blood of Jesus.

More good news! Jesus is the Healer. He is our sick offering. God gave His Son for the sickness and disease of the whole world. In the atonement, the effects or penalty of sin was paid for: sickness and disease, mental illness, poverty, and the second death. The prophet declared the healer. *"Surely he hath borne our sicknesses, and carried our pains: yet we did esteem him stricken, smitten of God, and afflicted. But he was wounded for our transgressions; he was bruised for our iniquities: the judgment of our peace was upon him; and with his scourging we are healed."* Isaiah 53:4-5. Jesus Christ bore our sins and our sicknesses. Through His blood sacrifice, He removed the power of both of these Adamic weaknesses. In England during World War II, there were bomb shelters for the civilians to flee to during Hitler's air raids. One lady went missing, and the authorities assumed she was dead. Rather she was home sleeping. She was asked, "Were you not afraid?" She replied, "No, I read the Bible. He neither slumbers nor sleeps…I thought it no need for both of us to stay awake." Likewise, our Lord Jesus bore our sins and our sicknesses.

Why should we bear either? By grace through faith, let's honor Him as our Savior/Healer.

Jesus is our atonement; at the cross, our sin and sickness were paid for. We see a type and picture of this great redemption in Numbers 21:6-9. The fiery serpents referred to in Numbers 21:6 denote sin and the effects of sin. In verse 7-9, God gives the provision for the power of the penalty of sin, the brass serpent. When it is set upon a pole and lifted, it denotes Jesus being lifted up on the cross. (Jesus referred to this type and picture recorded in John 3:14-15.) Sin and the penalty of sin have been judged. And as a man looks upon Jesus and His cross, considers it, examines it, and gazes upon it, he is forgiven and healed. Forgiven through the sin offering and healed through the sick offering; Jesus is our Savior/Healer!

Our two-fold redemption is seen in Isaiah 53:4-5, the forgiveness of our sin and the healing of our physical bodies. *"Surely He bore our grief or our sicknesses and carried our sorrows, our pains"*. *Borne* (Nasa, Hebrew) means to "suffer punishment for something with the result of removing it or taking it away." *"He has borne our sickness…"* Thus, Jesus bore our sickness vicariously; He suffered as our substitute for our sickness and disease. However, it's not magic; it's not mere head knowledge. You have to see Him as your healer. You have to seize that revelation. You have to say it and persist in it and you will eventually have it. Let's do it! *"He carried our pains…"* Carried is the Hebrew word Sabal which means to bear something as a penalty or a chastisement. Vicariously,

He bore our pains in penalty and in suffering. The Young's translation, *"surely our sicknesses he hath borne and our pains He hath carried them."* Then we have the gospel of Matthew Commentary on Isaiah 53:4: *"When the evening was come, they brought unto him many that were possessed with devils: and he cast out the spirits with his word, and healed all that were sick: That it might be fulfilled which was spoken by Esaias the prophet, saying, Himself took our infirmities, and bare our sicknesses"* Matthew 8:16,17.

Listed are other promises declaring the good news of our two-fold redemption. *"Bless the LORD, O my soul: and all that is within me, bless his holy name. Bless the LORD, O my soul, and forget not all his benefits: Who forgiveth all thine iniquities; who healeth all thy diseases; Who redeemeth thy life from destruction; who crowneth thee with loving-kindness and tender mercies."* Psalms 103:1-4. *"Who his own self bare our sins in his own body on the tree, that we, being dead to sins, should live unto righteousness: by whose stripes ye were healed."* I Peter 2:24.

Our two-fold redemption as seen in the gospels: *"Whether is it easier to say to the sick of the palsy, Thy sins be forgiven thee; or to say, Arise, and take up thy bed, and walk? But that ye may know that the Son of man hath power on earth to forgive sins, (he saith to the sick of the palsy,) I say unto thee, Arise, and take up thy bed, and go thy way into thine house."* Mark 2:9-11.

Our two-fold redemption as being ministered by the elders under the new covenant: *"Is any sick among you? Let him call for the elders of the church; and let them pray over him, anointing him with oil in the name of the Lord: And the prayer of faith shall save the sick, and the Lord shall raise him up; and if he have committed sins, they shall be forgiven him."* James 5:14,15.

Enclosed is an outline that I did over thirty years ago on God's will for divine health and healing. Read it, meditate on it, and confess it!

GOD'S WILL FOR DIVINE HEALTH AND HEALING

I. There are Great Promises to Those Who will Believe the Word of God:

II Peter 1:4 – "By which (knowing Jesus) are given to us (believers) exceedingly great and precious promises, that by these ye might be partakers of the Divine Nature…"

II Corinthians 1:20 – "For all the promises of God in him (Jesus) are yes and in him (Jesus) Amen, unto the glory of God by us."

II. The Exceedingly Great and Precious Promises of DIVINE HEALTH and HEALING:

Exodus 23:25 – "And ye shall serve the Lord your God, and He shall bless thy bread and thy water, and I will take sickness away from the midst of thee."

Psalms 103:2-3 – "Bless the Lord O my soul and forget

not all His benefits; who forgiveth <u>all thine iniquities</u> (sin): who healeth <u>ALL thy diseases</u>.

<u>Psalms 107:20</u> – "He sent his Word and <u>healed them</u>, and delivered them from destructions."

<u>Proverbs 4:20-22</u> – "My son, attend to my words; incline your ear unto my sayings. Let them (God's word) <u>not</u> depart from your eyes; <u>keep them</u> (God's word) in the midst of your heart. For they are <u>life</u> unto those that find them, and <u>health</u> (medicine) to <u>all their flesh</u>."

<u>Psalm 91:10</u> – "There shall <u>no</u> evil befall thee, neither shall <u>ANY</u> plague (disease) come nigh thy dwelling." <u>CONFESS IT!</u>

<u>Malachi 3:6</u> – "For I am the Lord, I change <u>NOT</u>…!"

III. For <u>ALL</u> the Promises of God in Him (Jesus) are <u>YES</u>…!

<u>Isaiah 53:4</u> – "Surely He hath borne our grief's (sicknesses) and carried our sorrows (pain); Yet we did esteem Him (Jesus) stricken, smitten of God and afflicted."

<u>Matthew 8:16,17</u> – "When the evening was come, they brought unto Him many that were possessed with demons and He cast out the spirits with his word, and <u>HEALED ALL</u> that were sick. That it might be fulfilled which was spoken by Isaiah the prophet, saying, He himself took our infirmities, and bore our sicknesses (on the cross).

<u>I Peter 2:24</u> – "Who his own self bore our sins in His own body on the tree: that we being dead to sins, should

live unto righteousness; by whose stripes you WERE HEALED!

I John 3:8 – "…for His purpose the Son of God was manifested – that He might destroy the works (sickness) of the devil."

Galatians 3:13 – "Christ has redeemed us from the curse of the law (include sickness) being made a curse for us."

Acts 10:38 – "God anointed Jesus of Nazareth with the Holy Ghost and with power: who went about doing GOOD, and HEALING ALL that were oppressed of the devil; for God was with Him."

Hebrews 13:8 – "Jesus Christ, the same yesterday and TODAY and forever."

IV. There are NO Exceptions to His Promises…!

I Kings 8:56 – "Blessed be the Lord, that hath given rest unto his people Israel, according to ALL that He promises: there has not failed ONE WORD of ALL his good promise."

Ezekiel 12:25 – "I am the Lord: I will speak and the WORD I shall speak shall come to pass: I say the WORD and WILL perform it, saith the Lord."

A. The Old Covenant of Healing:

Exodus 15:26 – "IF thou wilt diligently hearken to the voice of the Lord; and do that which is right in His sight; and will give ear to His commandments;

and keep all His statutes: I will put none of these diseases upon thee, which I brought upon the Eygptians: For I am the Lord that HEALETH THEE."

Covenant – A divine union between God and His people: God is the first party or elder partner and has committed Himself NEVER to break the promise of His covenant of agreement.

NOTE: All of God's people under the Old Covenant (Old Testament) had healing, deliverance, protection, and prosperity. We have a BETTER covenant or agreement with God, the NEW TESTAMENT.

B. The New Covenant of Healing, Salvation, etc."

Hebrews 8:6 – "But now He (Jesus) obtained a more excellent ministry, by how much also he is the mediator of a better covenant, which was established upon better promises."

Hebrews 8:10 – "For this is the covenant that I will make with the house of Israel after those days, saith the Lord; I will put my laws into their mind, and write them in their hearts; and I will be to them a God and they shall be to me a people.

Jesus said: "The Holy Ghost will teach you ALL THINGS, He will guide you into ALL TRUTH, and He shall glorify Me."

V. How to Embrace God's Exceeding Great Promises of God….
   A. Hear and BELIEVE the Word of God…
      Romans 10:17 – "Faith cometh by hearing and hearing by the word of God."
   B. Meditate on and personalize the promises of God…
      Proverbs 4:21 – "…keep them in the midst of your heart."
   C. Ask in the NAME OF JESUS…
      John 14:14, 15 – "And whatsoever (healing) ye ask in my NAME, I WILL DO IT!"
   D. Mark 11:24 – "Therefore I say unto you, what things so ever ye desire (healing) when ye pray, believe that ye RECEIVE them and YE SHALL HAVE THEM!"

CHAPTER EIGHT

Deliverance from the Stronghold of Rejection

Again, consider this truth to understand deliverance from darkness and demons: the mind is the place of demonic entrance, defeat, and destruction. We were once blinded in our minds by the dark god of this present world system. *"But if our gospel be hid, it is hid to them that are lost: In whom the god of this world hath blinded the minds of them which believe not, lest the light of the glorious gospel of Christ, who is the image of God, should shine unto them. For we preach not ourselves, but Christ Jesus the Lord; and ourselves your servants for Jesus' sake."* II Corinthians 4:3-5. We were blinded by the lust of our eyes: materialism, more and more of things that are passing away. We were blinded by the lust of our flesh: body appetites and the pleasures of sin; focusing on recreation, fads, and fashions. We were blinded by the pride of life: ambition, success, position, and recognition. But God, by the power of the Holy Ghost, convicted us of sin, judgment, and righteousness. By the grace of repentance, the Holy Ghost enlightened our minds to Him and His kingdom and we decided to follow Jesus. At the moment of our decision, as we turned from sin and death and turned to righteousness and life, we were regenerated. Our spirit man was born-again. In 1968, I repented under the convicting power of the Holy Ghost, that is, I had a change of mind of whose kingdom I would serve: the kingdom of darkness and death or the kingdom of light and life. I choose Jesus and was changed in a moment of time. Rejoice!!

Following our conversion, we entered into spiritual warfare. The demons and darkness are working against us to change our minds or regain control of our will and our decision making. Again, at the new birth our spirit-man was regenerated but not our minds. Our minds need deliverance and renewal through the enlightening word of God. The Christian struggle is in the mind. You have heard this statement of truth before, "The Battlefield is the Mind." Evil spirits war against truth in the mind. We live in a world at war with our minds. It is not a cultural war or a political war rather it is a spiritual war geared to blind and bind us. So therefore, the weapons of our warfare cannot be worldly or carnal. The weapons of our warfare have divine power to destroy or drive out the demonic strongholds. II Corinthians 10:3,4. Again, strongholds are negative thought patterns that are set-in to control the mind and bring defeat and despair. There are rebellious thoughts, lustful thoughts, rejection thoughts, bitter thoughts, jealous thoughts, failure and fear thoughts. The negative thought list is too numerous to mention. The good news is that we have grace and authority in our Lord Jesus to *"destroy every negative argument and proud obstacle that exalts itself against the knowledge of God and we are able to take every thought captive to obey Christ."* II Corinthians 10:5.

For example, my oldest daughter, Lynne Aguillard Venus, was stricken with a bi-polar stronghold. In her forty-fourth year of life, in a depressed state, the spirit of suicide overtook her mind and she committed suicide in my bedroom while we were away from home. The next day, as I laid in bed grieving, thoughts began to flood my mind: "You should have done this; you shouldn't have done that; you could have been home." On and on the negative and dark thoughts flooded my mind and tormented me. Finally, I realized that this wasn't the Holy Ghost speaking to me. I was under a demonic and dark attack to move me out of the grace of God. Immediately, I took authority and in Jesus' name I destroyed every high and negative thought that had exalted itself against the knowledge of my heavenly Father. As a daddy, by the grace of God, I did my best. My daughter was a casualty of war, a victim of a demonic bi-polar stronghold. Listen to me believer; the Holy Spirit is not the voice of condemnation and guilt. Rather, He is the voice of comfort, acceptance, and life in Jesus name.

I will repeat a truth so you can gear-up and grace-up to win the day: Satan has access to your mind. The darkness and the demons have the power to communicate to us through our thoughts organ, *"But I fear, lest by any means, as the serpent beguiled Eve through his subtilty, so your minds should be corrupted from the simplicity that is in Christ."* II Corinthians 11:3. Accusations, temptations, condemnation, and thoughts are inseparable. Evil spirits have power to project deceiving and destructive thoughts into the believer's mind, *"But Peter said, Ananias, why hath Satan filled thine heart to lie to the Holy Ghost, and to keep back part of the price of the land?"* Acts 5:3. Any unwary believer can be bound up and hindered and hurt through negative thought strongholds. In personal deliverance and counseling, we have the Christ given authority to pull out the fiery darts and oppression of demon spirits in the mental and even physical areas.

In my early years of understanding the power of deliverance in setting the captives free, I share with you the following testimony. Right after being spirit filled in 1975, a young lady in my church was under a serious demonic bondage, oppressed to the point that her eyes were glazed. She was under a stronghold of depression and despair. In my small twelve by twelve foot office, Apostle Jim Clark ministered deliverance to her. I saw the power of God set a captive free! It was a divine encounter that impregnated me with a vision and faith to set captives free. Over the course of my personal ministry I have seen hundreds set free to the glory of God. Jesus said, *"But if I cast out devils by the Spirit of God, then the kingdom of God is come unto you."* Matthew 12:28.

In conclusion, I am going to expose one kind of negative thought: rejection. Unless you were raised in an atmosphere of a warm, loving home and church body, you have been troubled by the dark thoughts of rejection and self-rejection. Rejection is a thought impression that you are always on the outside looking inside. Rejection is a mindset that you do not feel like you are a vital part of a church body or even of your own family. A rejection personality withdraws itself; no ability to be transparent or let anybody into your life. A rejection personality is full of timidity; tends to be a loner. A rejection personality is easily offended; takes all correction as rejection.

Two Main Roots or Causes of Rejection Strongholds in the Mind of the Individual

1. **First and foremost, a wounded childhood.** Overly-strict parents; harsh and demanding. Always speaking down to the child or children. Angry and harsh words contain rejection, they are words of death.

   Then there are permissive parents who spare the rod, that is they failed to instruct and correct. They failed to set proper boundaries and keep a child's heart in alignment with the heart of our heavenly Father. This produces children that are out of control. They are misfits, rejected by those around them and as a result are full of self-rejection. A permissive atmosphere has no love and care in it and is probably a worse atmosphere for rejection strongholds than the overly-strict parents.

In a wounded childhood, there are parents with an unwanted pregnancy. The child is rejected in the womb and rejection becomes part of their DNA. Then there are parents caught up in materialism, busy making money to buy more and more stuff that can't really give life or acceptance. I call them missing in action parents, or MIA's.; parents that make no time to attend their child's sporting event or school program; have no time to sit down and listen to their child's setbacks or achievements; or parents that have no time to play or even pray with their children. Many parents have been missing in action. As a result, that carries a wound, filling a child's mind with rejection and bitterness.

For example, my wife had a dad who never hugged her, kissed her or affirmed her. She carried a father's wound and a spirit of rejection in her mind. In our early twenties, she encountered Jesus and the Holy Ghost set her free from the stronghold of rejection and anger. By the power of God, she is one of the most loving and free-giving individuals that you will ever meet. In the next chapter, I will share deliverances for offenses, wounds, and a root of bitterness or anger.

Also a broken home with divorced parents who fought and used their children in their battleground of differences is an open door to the demonic stronghold of rejection and bitterness.

2. A second major area is to be wounded by words.
"Death and life are in the power of the tongue: and they that love it shall eat the fruit thereof." Proverbs 18:21.
There are children and teenagers that can maliciously

hurt and wound a classmate with negative words. At our Christian school, we forbid name calling and would discipline children who were guilty of malicious words or name calling. As a child, I remember a boy who wore thick glasses, and uncaring classmates would call him "Four Eyes," thus rejection. Another teenager had a rather large head, a few uncaring students called him "Buffalo Head," thus rejection. My oldest brother, as a teenager, was overweight. Some of his peers would call him "Fatso," thus rejection. One young lady whom I knew well was maliciously teased by a high school teacher who called her, "Short and stout like a little teapot." This ministered a stronghold of rejection which later manifested in an eating disorder. Uncaring words will wound and become an open door to darkness and demons. God help us to be kind and minister words of love and acceptance. Very briefly, I listed a spiritual diagnosis of a rejection. (Some of these thoughts were read from a book, *"Pigs in the Palor"* by Frank and Ida Mae Hammon.)

The Active Side of the Rejection Personality

Rebellious, stubborn, and self-willed. Envy and resentment of someone else's success. Tries to control and possess; very possessive in a close friendship. A root of bitterness, explosive behavior at any offense or towards anyone that crosses their will. Note: If you have these symptoms, you may need the help of a deliverance counselor.

The Passive Side of a Rejection Personality

Self-rejection and fear of rejection are the main expressions of a stronghold of rejection.

Sexual lust: the love need is trying to be satisfied through sexual relationships with the opposite sex. For example, a love-starved daughter who has seldom been affirmed by daddy will seek male companionship to fill in that great love need. And often, will fall into premature sex.

Insecurity, inferiority, and timidity. In this there is also an attitude of unworthiness and a sense of failure. Sometimes a rejected mindset will express failures and shortcomings over and over.

Finally, on the passive side of rejection personality is false compassion and false responsibility. For example, a rejection type personality will over-do church activity while neglecting their own family. Inordinate affection for animals; humanizing cats and dogs.

Note: If you have these symptoms, you may need the help of a deliverance/counselor.

In conclusion, there are four basic steps in beginning your deliverance from the stronghold of rejection:

1. **Repent of rejection and self rejection**. It is a demonic and selfish pattern of behavior. Therefore, it is sinful and degrading. Repent, turn from it, renounce it, and receive the blood of Jesus cleansing your mind from all rejection, self rejection, and self pity. Close the door!

2. **Come and kneel at the cross of Jesus**. At the cross,

He bore your rejection that you might receive the full acceptance of your Heavenly Father. *"He is despised and rejected of men; a man of sorrows, and acquainted with grief: and we hid as it were our faces from him; he was despised, and we esteemed him not."* *"Yet it pleased the LORD to bruise him; he hath put him to grief: when thou shalt make his soul an offering for sin, he shall see his seed, he shall prolong his days, and the pleasure of the LORD shall prosper in his hand."* Isaiah 53:3,10. Start It pleased here…It pleased the Father to bruise Him; to crush Him; to reject Him; He was crucified, totally rejected, and buried by wicked men. Start He was br*uised here…He was bruised. Jesus Christ bore your wounds, your hurts, and all the years of your rejection.*

3. **By faith, receive and confess the exchange of the cross.** Get on *your knees and receivE The love and full acceptance of your Lord Jesus. He fully loves you and accepts you as you are and He will change you into His image!* *"The praise of the glory of his gRACE, wherein he hath made us accepted in the beloved."* Ephesians 1:6.

Accepted: You are an object, a person of your heavenly Father's loving care and full attention; you are highly favored; *"He delivers you because he delights in you."* Period!

Accepted: The blood of our Lord Jesus atoned; it paid

for your sin of rejection. Therefore, receive it, you are free to love yourself and love others in Jesus name.

4. **Repent of all bitterness and resentment toward your offenders.** (I will share this in detail in the next chapter.)

By an act of your will, out loud forgive your offenders one by one, everyone who has wounded you with words or through their actions or inaction.

Then, command the spirits of bitterness and resentment and anger to leave your mind in Jesus' name. Give glory to God in your deliverance and freedom. Tell others.

Note: You still may need follow up with a deliverance counselor.

CHAPTER NINE

Overcoming Offenses: Deliverance from the Root of Bitterness

Everyone must realize this reality: offenses will come. Jesus said, *"Woe unto the world because of offenses, for it must needs be that offenses come..."* Matthew 18:7. Offense is a stumbling block, a carefully laid trap of the devil. *Offense* means "to be hurt, to be wronged or to be accused wrongly." The Webster's Dictionary defines an *offense* as "an attack; a happening that often causes anger or resentment." An offense can be caused by rejection. I pastored for thirty-seven years. I have seen hundreds come and go. I have felt the pain of hundreds leaving. Often, I heard the departing words, "I love you but I have to leave!" By the grace of God I overcame rejection over and over again and learned to stay free of bitterness.

Again, offenses are certain, but the real issue is how you deal with them. A pastor by the name of Larry Lea gave this

three step progress of bondage to an offense:
1. "If you nurse it and focus on it…"
2. "If you rehearse it, repeat it over and over to yourself and others."
3. "It will curse you…you will become the victim of a root of anger and bitterness."

Unresolved anger and bitterness give opportunity to the devil. *"Be ye angry, and sin not: let not the sun go down upon your wrath: Neither give place to the devil"* Ephesians 4:26,27. In other words, don't give opportunity to the devil. Don't let an offense or anger give jurisdiction to the devil to divide relationships. "Esteem your relationship greater than your issues." (Ron Corizen) My wife and I have a little dog named Jackie. She is a white short-haired Jack Russell that sheds hair. One night I was having dinner on a T.V. table in our den when I noticed white dog hair on the wool rug near my feet. Out of my aversion for detached dog hair, I told my wife that Jackie had to go. The shedding of dog hair near my dinner was ruining my appetite. She responded, "No, I am covenant with our dog." I replied, "I am not covenant with dogs only people, Jackie has to go." Then the tears started and it caused me not to press my case. In silence, I heard a truth that I was taught, "Esteem your relationship more than your issues or differences." Case closed, Jackie is still with us and there is peace in my home.

Unresolved differences and anger give demon powered

arguments to war against your home or church. Unresolved anger or bitterness is sinful and divisive. *"But if ye have bitter envying and strife in your hearts, glory not, and lie not against the truth. This wisdom descendeth not from above, but is earthly, sensual, devilish. For where envying and strife is, there is confusion and every evil work."* James 3:14-16.

I am going to share three truths that will set you free from offenses coupled with the root of anger and bitterness:

1. **Repent!** Anger and bitterness is fleshly sin. It has the power to damn your soul. Read Galatians 6:19-21 which I refer to as the roll call of Hell. In this list is adultery, fornication, drunkenness, and murder. These are obvious hell-sending sins. But along with this list is anger, strife and divisions.

2. **Forgiveness:** This is the second key to your deliverance from anger and the root of bitterness. The Lord commands it. *"Let all bitterness, and wrath, and anger, and clamour, and evil speaking, be put away from you, with all malice. "And be ye kind one to another, tenderhearted, forgiving one another, even as God for Christ's sake hath forgiven you."* Ephesians 4:31,32. Forgiveness means to let it go! Throw away your scorecard. Before I left my home church to go to a theological seminary, I had fought against a deacon. During the business meetings, this particular deacon would stand against my pastor. I was offended for my pastor and held deep resentment towards this out of

order deacon. In my morning devotions, the Holy Spirit quickened Matthew 5:44, *"But I say unto you, Love your enemies, bless them that curse you, do good to them that hate you, and pray for them which despitefully use you, and persecute you."* I obeyed and began to pray for the confronting deacon. When I left the church for the seminary, he was one of the men I loved the most. The power of prayer and forgiveness drove bitterness out of my heart and gave me a great capacity to love the offender. As we consider forgiveness as a basic key in our deliverance from the darkness of anger and bitterness, listed are five motivations for forgiveness:

a.) Forgiveness is not only the centerpiece of the cross; it is also the centerpiece of our personal freedom to love God and to love others. It is vertical freedom. *"If we say that we have no sin, we deceive ourselves, and the truth is not in us. If we confess our sins, he is faithful and just to forgive us our sins, and to cleanse us from all unrighteousness"* I John 1:8-9. I am a blood breather. I breathe sin out when I confess my short comings and I breathe the cleansing blood of Jesus in, filling and cleansing my soul.

b.) Second motivation to forgive is recorded in Matthew 6:12, *"And forgive us our debts, as we forgive our debtors."* This is a truth! When you refuse to forgive your spouse, friend, employer, co-worker or relative, you are asking God not to forgive you!

Selfish anger or bitterness is not worth your peace or forgiveness with God your Father. The real test of your relationship with God is to forgive others. *"For if ye forgive men their trespasses, your heavenly Father will also forgive you: But if ye forgive not men their trespasses, neither will your Father forgive your trespasses."* Matthew 6:14-15.

c.) Third motivation for forgiveness is the divine link to heart faith. There are two basic keys to heart faith that moves mountains of difficulties. The first is a heartfelt decree, *"Verily I say unto you, That whosoever shall say unto this mountain, Be thou removed, and be thou cast into the sea; and shall not doubt in his heart, but shall believe that those things which he saith shall come to pass; he shall have whatsoever he saith. Therefore I say unto you, What things soever ye desire, when ye pray, believe that ye receive them, and ye shall have them."* Mark 11:23-24. The second key is to forgive, to let it go, *"And when ye stand praying, forgive, if ye have ought against any: that your Father also which is in heaven may forgive you your trespasses"* Matthew 11:25. The life of faith hangs onto a spirit of forgiveness and the confession of God's word.

d.) Fourth motivation to forgiveness is to escape the tormentors. Read Matthew 18:21-35. In this parable, our Lord Jesus taught unlimited forgiveness.

Forgive seven times seventy. In this picture of truth, the forgiven was unforgiving and he was cast into prison. Jesus told us that if we don't forgive, then He would turn us over to the tormentors. *"Shouldest not thou also have had compassion on thy fellowservant, even as I had pity on thee? And his lord was wroth, and delivered him to the tormentors, till he should pay all that was due unto him So likewise shall my heavenly Father do also unto you, if ye from your hearts forgive not every one his brother their trespasses."* Matthew 18:33-35. In 1980, I was on a mission trip to Bangkok, Thailand. During that stay, I had a difference with a fellow traveling pastor and raised my voice at him in anger. That night, the Holy Spirit turned me over to the tormentors because of my unrepented anger. I was so tormented, full of fear and mental anguish, that I would have taken drugs for relief. In the midst of my crying out, the Lord spoke to me, "Don't you ever raise your voice to one of my servants again." I said, yes, in deep repentance and immediately I was delivered from the tormentors. That happened over thirty years ago, never again have I raised my voice in anger against one of His servants. Thank God for the gift of repentance and His immediate forgiveness and great deliverance.

e.) Fifth motivation to forgive is to see the danger of

eternal judgment. *"Follow peace with all men, and holiness, without which no man shall see the Lord: Looking diligently lest any man fail of the grace of God; lest any root of bitterness springing up trouble you, and thereby many be defiled."* Hebrews 12:14-15. Follow peace, be in a right relationship with all men; no walls of anger or resentment. Then, stay in the grace and forgiveness of God, lest an offense and a root of bitterness defile you. You can't take bitterness to heaven. Forgive and let it go!

In review, the first two steps to freedom from the offense of anger and bitterness is to: *Repent*, of anger and bitterness as a fleshly sin. Secondly: *Forgive*, the Lord commands it!

The third step is *Deliverance*. In the spirit of repentance and forgiveness, the stronghold of bitterness has lost its legal right to oppress you. At this point, cast out the spirits of anger, resentment, and bitterness. I recommend that you have a pastor or one of his approved leaders to assist you in casting out this bitterness stronghold. In the process of deliverance, the Holy Ghost surgically removes the root of bitterness. Once this cancer is out, you will experience freedom. Freedom to love God with all your heart, freedom to love yourself, and freedom to love all people in Jesus' name!

CHAPTER TEN

Deliverance from Sexual Oppression and Guilt

The liberal media is bombarding our minds with sexual immorality. Jezebel is running Hollywood and corrupting the minds of millions, believers and unbelievers. What blinds the lost, blinds the saved. God help us to overcome the sexual barrage and perversions of the evil one. There are three main areas of sexual sin and open doors for demonic oppression. *"And lest, when I come again, my God will humble me among you, and that I shall bewail many which have sinned already, and have not repented of the uncleanness and fornication and lasciviousness which they have committed."* II Corinthians 12:21.

1. **The first open door is uncleaness:** this means to be impure; filth, lewd and foul. Uncleaness is a scriptural term for homosexuality and other sexual perversions. *"Wherefore God also gave them up to uncleanness*

through the lusts of their own hearts, to dishonour their own bodies between themselves." Romans 1:24. Homosexuality is at the bottom of the barrel of sexual perversion. It is unthinkable that the President of the United States, the Supreme Court, and most of the nation has embraced same-sex marriage as a normal lifestyle to be enforced by law on the general public. At this writing, eight states have legalized same-sex marriage. This is ungodly and unthinkable in a nation with a Christian heritage. I smell the smoke of Sodom and Gomorrah. A city, region or nation that approves homosexuality or same-sex marriage is at the striking point of God's wrath and judgment. Harvard sociologist, Pitrim Sorokin, analyzed cultures spanning thousands of years on several different continents and found that virtually no society that ceased to define marriage as a union between man and woman survived. Unless the body of Christ wakes up and our pulpits thunder with righteousness, our nation is going down a path of doom and destruction. If you are a homosexual, the power of the blood of Jesus and the Holy Ghost can set you free!

2. **Fornication is a door for demonic blindness and oppression.** Fornication is sexual immorality; indulging in unlawful lust. In its base meaning, it is illegal sexual intercourse. There are three main areas of fornication.

   a.) Premarital sex: The latest survey indicated that approximately 70% of senior high school students are sexually active. Hollywood, with its thousands of bedroom scenes, has done its deep immoral work. Jezebel is the seducer. The Federal government promotes teen promiscuity with free condoms and humanistic sex education classes. The church as a whole is too weak and wimpy to address this critical sin issue. The bible teaches abstinence until marriage. Most public schools, state, and national government leaders reject and scorn this approach. Therefore, the multitude of pregnant unmarried teenagers will often abort unwanted babies. Abortion is horrendous. We are murdering 1.2 million unborn babies per year. From one end to the other, our land is full of innocent blood. Their innocent blood is crying out from the ground for the justice of God. Just based on abortion alone, America is a nation under judgment. God help the pulpits to thunder with righteousness and deliver a generation from the power of sexual sin.

b.) Incest is having sex within the family circle. *"Cursed is anyone who sleeps with his sister, the daughter of his father or the daughter of his mother. Then all the people shall say, 'Amen!' Cursed is anyone who sleeps with his mother-in-law. Then all the people shall say, 'Amen!'"* Deuteronomy 27:22-23. Those who commit such sexual sins come under a curse. Demons inflict and carry out the curses of the broken moral law. Therefore, incest is an open door to demonic intrusion. The name of Jesus and the blood of Jesus will set the repentive captive free from darkness and demons.

c.) Adultery is to have an extra-marital affair. *"But whoso committeth adultery with a woman lacketh understanding: he that doeth it destroyeth his own soul. A wound and dishonour shall he get; and his reproach shall not be wiped away."* Proverbs 6:32-33. Over the forty-four years of my ministry, I have counseled more than a few couples entangled and divided by the sin of adultery. It is soul ripping and the rejection of the sacred trust of sexual purity between a husband and wife. Adultery violates the marriage bed with impurity. The innocent partner need not give themselves to sexual intercourse with the adulterer or adulteress or that individual partakes of the sexual impurity. The guilty partner must come into a spirit of repentance, deliverance, and restoration to restore the purity of the marriage relationship.

3. **The third open door is lasciviousness.** Lasciviousness denotes excess or absence of restraint a preoccupation with the body or sexual pleasures, excessive or unrestrained physical excitement. This moves into sexual addiction. Surveys indicate that one out of three men are sexual addicts. It is an epidemic in the lost world and even in the body of Christ. Again, Hollywood and Jezebel, the pornography industry has done its deep diabolical work. Among men, masturbation coupled

with sexual fantasy or pornography is a main open door for darkness and demonic intrusion. As the Senior Overseer of the Network of Related Pastors, I have dealt with pastors who have become sexual addicts. Usually it is pornography coupled with masturbation. In most cases, the lead pastor has to be set down and assigned to a sexual addiction counselor for deliverance and freedom. It is a long process of counseling and restoration. If the pastor is repentive, freedom will come over an extended period, usually nine months to a year. Jesus Christ came to destroy the works of the devil. A major area of destroying the works of the devil is pornography and sexual addiction.

Four Symptoms of Sexual Oppression

1. **Strife in the spirit:** *"From whence come wars and fightings among you? Come they not hence, even of your lusts that war in your members? Ye lust, and have not: ye kill, and desire to have, and cannot obtain: ye fight and war, yet ye have not, because ye ask not."* James 4:1-2. A lustful person or an individual in sexual sin usually has a stubborn and unteachable spirit. Often, easily moved towards being angry and is argumentative.

2. **Justifier:** "I have needs. I am free to do as I please in my private life. Anyway, most men are doing it." *"For there are certain men crept in unawares, who were before of old ordained to this condemnation, ungodly*

men, turning the grace of our God into lasciviousness, and denying the only Lord God, and our Lord Jesus Christ." Jude 1:4. A side note: More and more women are getting caught in the trap of pornography and sexual addictions. A growing and alarming number of lesbians.

3. **Rebellious towards authority.** *"The Lord knoweth how to deliver the godly out of temptations, and to reserve the unjust unto the day of judgment to be punished: But chiefly them that walk after the flesh in the lust of uncleanness, and despise government. Presumptuous are they, self-willed, they are not afraid to speak evil of dignities."* II Peter 2:9-10. Most unrepentative sex addicts do not honor civil or spiritual authority. They are self-willed and unteachable.

4. **Torments of guilt and condemnation rob the individual of the peace and joy of heaven.** There is no anointing of faith to believe and receive the blessings of God's kingdom. *"Beloved, if our heart condemn us not, then have we confidence toward God."* John 3:21. A guilty heart and a condemned mind cannot move in the faith of God. But the blood of Jesus, *"If we confess our sins, he is faithful and just to forgive us our sins, and to cleanse us from all unrighteousness."* I John 1:9.

Deliverance from the Darkness of Demon Oppression in the Sexual Area

1. Close the open door of sin. Repent and receive God's forgiveness.

2. Renounce the unclean spirits and command them to leave in Jesus' name. Most often, the sexually oppressed need ministry to counsel them and walk them through deliverance.

3. Bring your body into subjection through prayer and fasting.

4. Cultivate the fear of the Lord. Be in constant awareness that God is watching and evaluating everything we say or do. *"For the ways of man are before the eyes of the LORD, and he pondereth all his goings. His own iniquities shall take the wicked himself, and he shall be holden with the cords of his sins."* Proverbs 5:21-22

5. Whatever you do, do it all for the glory of God. Every decision you make, do it to glorify God. *"Whether therefore ye eat, or drink, or whatsoever ye do, do all to the glory of God."* I Corinthians 10:31.

6. Forget those things behind you. Your past will not determine your future. His presence and purpose in your life will.

7. Finally, by morning, sit at the feet of Jesus and get the Word of God into your heart. *"Wherewithal shall a young man cleanse his way? By taking heed thereto according to thy word."* Psalms 119:9,11.

Chapter Eleven

Breaking the Curses

There are four basic purposes of our Lord's first coming.

1. **To redeem man:** The blood of Jesus redeems us. The blood of Jesus sets us free from the power of sin, Satan, and selfishness. Thank God for the shed blood of Jesus!

2. **To reconcile man:** To bring us back into the Father's fellowship, favor, and friendship. *"To wit, that God was in Christ, reconciling the world unto himself, not imputing their trespasses unto them; and hath committed unto us the word of reconciliation."* II Corinthians 5:19.

3. **To restore man:** What the first Adam lost, the second Adam has won back through the power of the cross. He has all power and dominion and has delegated it to the going or obedient body of Christ.

4. **Jesus came to destroy or undo the works of the devil.**

"He that committeth sin is of the devil; for the devil sinneth from the beginning. For this purpose the Son of God was manifested, that he might destroy the works of the devil." I John 3:8.

In deliverance from darkness and demons, there are four truths in which all believers can be in agreement.

1. **The mind is the battlefield.** Evil spirits have access to our minds. The spiritual world operates through the thought realm. Temptations and oppression come in thought form. *"But I fear...as the serpent beguiled Eve through his subtly, so your minds should be corrupted from the simplicity that is in Christ."* II Corinthians 11:2,3.

2. **A believer can have a stronghold.** Strongholds are areas of fortified negative thinking. Evil spirits work through the thought realm to form oppressive strongholds in the human mind. *"...the weapons of our warfare are not carnal, but mighty through God to the pulling down of strongholds...casting down imaginations and every high thing that exalteth itself against the knowledge of God..."* II Corinthians 10:3-5.

3. **We as believers have an anointing to destroy and break the strongholds of darkness, demons, and disease.** *"How God anointed Jesus of Nazareth with the Holy Ghost and with power: who went about doing*

good, and healing all that were oppressed of the devil; for God was with him." Acts 10:38.

4. **Finally, curses are real.** There are four curses of the broken law. The curses of poverty, mental torment, sickness and diseases, and the second death. Evil spirits carry out the curses of the broken law.

The reality of a curse. It is possible for you or a family member to be under the power of a curse. Common natural terms: I am jinxed; snake bit; it never goes right; bad luck. The person under a cloud of despair and depression is often a result of the invisible hand of a curse. In my forty-four years of ministry, I have seen a certain sickness and disease follow a family line. Mental illness can be the invisible hand of a generational curse. For example, in my wife's family line there is a history of mental illness and suicides. She had an aunt and an uncle that committed suicide. One of her grandmother's in the same family line went to bed depressed in her mid-forties staying in that condition until her death almost fifty years later. Her mother stayed in and out of bi-polar breakdowns. The bi-polar curse came on our oldest daughter at the early age of twenty-two. The scripture teaches that a curse cannot come without cause. *"As the bird by wandering, as the swallow by flying, so the curse causeless shall not come."* Proverbs 26:2. In a marriage conflict, she became bitter and resentful. It was the open door for the generational curse of mental illness. Tragically her life ended in suicide at the young age of forty-four.

Again, Proverbs 25:2 states, *"...a curse cannot come with cause..."* There are eight basic open doors to curses that can be closed by repentance, renouncing, and closing the open door.

1. **The open door of idolatry**...worshipping other gods, statues, relics, etc. *"Thou shalt not make unto thee any graven image, or any likeness of anything that is in heaven above, or that is in the earth beneath, or that is in the water under the earth. Thou shalt not bow down thyself to them, nor serve them: for I the LORD thy God am a jealous God, visiting the iniquity of the fathers upon the children unto the third and fourth generation of them that hate me; And shewing mercy unto thousands of them that love me, and keep my commandments."* Exodus 20:4-6.

2. **The open door of dishonoring your parents**. *"Honour thy father and mother; which is the first commandment with promise; That it may be well with thee, and thou mayest live long on the earth."* Ephesians 6:2-3.

3. **The open door of incest.** Twenty-five percent of American teenage girls are molested by their dads. That means one in four of American fathers are under a curse. *"Cursed be he that lieth with his father's wife; because he uncovereth his father's skirt. And all the people shall say, Amen. Cursed be he that lieth with his sister, the daughter of his father, or the daughter of his mother. And all the people shall say, Amen. Cursed be he that*

lieth with his mother in law. And all the people shall say, Amen." Deuteronomy 27:20, 22-23.

4. **The open door of occult practices.** I was ministering the Baptism of the Holy Spirit to a lady that was unable to receive. By word of knowledge, I questioned her about participating in the occult. She admitted to fortune tellers and horoscopes. This caused a spiritual blockage, she repented and closed this open door of oppression and freely received the Baptism of the Holy Spirit.

   Another lady had a spirit of infirmity against her physical body. As we prayed for her, it was revealed that she had practiced self-hypnosis, an occult practice. She repented of this sin, closed the open door, and was instantly healed. Glory to God! Deuteronomy 18:9-12 lists the occult practices. You can be set free from darkness, demons and disease.

5. **Rebellion against spiritual authority or the abuse of spiritual authority is sin and is an open door to a curse.** Miriam's rebellion against Moses as her spiritual authority. She was struck with the curse of leprosy. Numbers 12:1-10. Then there is Korah's rebellion against Moses. He and his henchmen were swallowed up by the earth. Numbers 16:1. The word of God exhorts: *"Obey your spiritual leaders and submit to them for they are constantly keeping watch over your souls and guarding your spiritual welfare..."* Hebrews

13:17. Apostolic and pastoral authority over your life is a protection from the afflictions and curses of demons.

Then there is the abuse of spiritual authority which is an open door to deception and failure. There have been situations where five-fold ministry has moved into pride and legalism. In such cases, the deceived authority lord's over God's people and begins to lock their free-will. Often movements and churches die because of the abuse or the lack of spiritual authority.

6. **Spoken curses.** One spoken curse is recorded in Genesis 31:32, *"With whomsoever thou findest thy gods, let him not live: before our brethren discern thou what is thine with me, and take it to thee. For Jacob knew not that Rachel had stolen them."* The background is that Rachel stole her father Laban's gods. As Rachel's father Laban approached, Jacob spoke death to the thief. Later, Rachel died in childbirth. The invisible hand of a spoken curse.

The scripture teaches, *"Death and life are in the power of the tongue: and they that love it shall eat the fruit thereof."* Proverbs 18:21. Words are containers. They contain life or death. You can speak a blessing over someone or you can speak a curse. There are curses spoken by parents: to a child, "You will never amount to anything." The parent spoke a curse of failure, an inability to succeed in life. A dad or mother can speak a curse over a child, "You are stupid!" The parent cursed their child with an inability to learn.

7. **Curses spoken by a third party like a coach, a teacher, a brother or sister.** For example, a high school teacher teased one of my daughters about her size. She was short but not really fat and just had an athletic build. He would call her teapot….short and stout. Under that confession she came under the curse of an eating disorder. She was driven to deprive herself of food to wear a size two dress. It almost destroyed her physical and mental life. Jesus delivered her from the darkness and deception of a serious eating disorder.

8. **Generational curses:** The curse is passed down through family lines and generational sin. This was explained earlier in the Reality of curses.

In conclusion, I bring good news that through Jesus Christ, God has provided a remedy for curses. At the cross, Jesus became a curse for us; he took on our sin and the penalty or curses of sin. *"Christ hath redeemed us from the curse of the law, being made a curse for us: for it is written, Cursed is every one that hangeth on a tree."* Galatians 3:13.

-At the cross, He was made sin with our sinfulness that we might be made righteous with His righteousness. *""For he hath made him to be sin for us, who knew no sin; that we might be made the righteousness of God in him."* II Corinthians 5:21.

-At the cross, He was made sick with our sickness that we might be made whole with His healing and health. *"Surely he hath borne our griefs, and carried our sorrows: yet we did esteem him stricken, smitten of God, and afflicted."* Isaiah 53:4.

-At the cross He took our fears, our worries, our anxieties, and our mental torment that we might have His peace in our spirit and mind. *"But he was wounded for our transgressions, he was bruised for our iniquities: the judgment of our peace was upon him; and with his stripes we are healed."* Isaiah 53:5.

-At the cross, He took our poverty that we might have His provision and wealth. *For ye know the grace of our Lord Jesus Christ, that, though he was rich, yet for your sakes he became poor, that ye through his poverty might be rich."* II Corinthians 8:9.

-At the cross, He took our wrath that we might have His favor and blessings on our life and on everything we do, victory and success. *"Yet it pleased the LORD to bruise him; he hath put him to grief: when thou shalt make his soul an offering for sin..."* Isaiah 53:10.

Therefore, as you embrace the victory of the cross, repent of the sin and the open door of the curse. As you repent, you receive the cleansing power of the blood and the power of the curse is broken. *"For whosoever shall call upon the name of the Lord shall be delivered."* Romans 10:13.

Chapter Twelve

Freedom: Keeping Your Mind Protected

Again, evil spirits have access to your mind. They have the power to inject negative thoughts—thoughts of fear, failure, doubt, discouragement, resentment, lust, and rejection. The list of negative thinking is too numerous to list. When the negative thoughts outweigh the positive, despair, depression, and hopelessness become the state of the mind. Keeping your mind free from the negative is the key to staying in the rest and peace of God.

The scripture is clear, *"For as a man thinketh, so is he..."* Proverbs 23:7. "If your thinking is wrong, your believing is wrong. So you must think God's thoughts. Wrong thinking and right believing don't work together." (Mike Ware). Therefore, demons and darkness war against your mind to put a bushel over it and block your flow of freedom, joy, peace, and righteousness in the Holy Ghost.

Negative thoughts received in our mind will keep the treasures of the kingdom of God from flowing through you. Here are examples of the fiery darts of the wicked one: "You are a loser! No one loves you! You are unlovely! You are a reject! You are not forgiven! You are unworthy! There is no blessing of God or favor of God on your life." God expects us to control our thought life. You must discern the suggestions that enter your mind. *"God's thoughts toward you are not evil or negative but thoughts of life and peace to give you a future and hope."* Jeremiah 29:11. The Holy Spirit does not give you suggestions of lust or suggestions of guilt and condemnation, despair or hopelessness. Jesus said, *"...I came that they may have life and enjoy life and have it in abundance to the full, till it overflows."* John 10:10.

There are five basic spiritual disciplines in keeping your mind protected and maintaining your freedom from darkness and demons.

1. **Live a disciplined life; no laziness or passivity.** An undisciplined life is an open door to demonic or negative thoughts. *"Keep thy heart with all diligence; for out of it are the issues of life."* Proverbs 4:23. Keep your ear gates. Refuse the garbage of someones negative thoughts about you or others. *"Put away from you false and dishonest speech."* Proverbs 4:24. Discipline your eyes; they are the gates to your mind. *"Let your eyes look directly forward..."* Proverbs 4:25. Discipline your feet. Plan your day, have a to-do list. Daily go with purpose and direction. *"Take heed to the path of your*

feet..." Proverbs 4:26. In living a disciplined life, you will have power to keep your heart with all diligence. For out of your heart flow the issues of life, courage and conviction, joy and peace, dreams and visions, conscience and worship.

2. **By morning, sit at the feet of our Lord Jesus.** In the morning, be still and know God. At day break, I get me a cup of coffee and go into the secret place to wait on the Lord and meditate in His Word. At His feet, I experience divine osmosis. I absorb the grace and the strength of the Holy Spirit. I receive grace to see the will of God, to be the will of God, and then to do the will of God. As you sit at the feet of Jesus, an exchange takes place. *"But they that wait upon the LORD shall renew their strength; they shall mount up with wings as eagles; they shall run, and not be weary; and they shall walk, and not faint."* Isaiah 40:31. At the feet of Jesus, you renew your strength: You give Him your human strength in exchange for His divine strength. By morning, God will be like the dew of the morning to you. *"I will be like the dew unto Israel..."* Hosea 14:5. The dew replenishes and refreshes the earth, the grass and all the vegetation. Dew does not fall in the heat of the day or when there is wind. Dew falls in the still and cool of the night. God's dew or refreshing falls on us as we wait on the Lord. By morning, I get grace to be a great husband and a godly father. I receive grace to be a spiritual father to pastors

and a prophet to the body and to the nation.

3. **A third basic step in protecting your mind is renewal.** We must think like God thinks. If we think like the world, we will not walk in the faith of God or in the freedom of the Holy Spirit. *"I beseech you therefore, brethren, by the mercies of God, that ye present your bodies a living sacrifice, holy, acceptable unto God, which is your reasonable service. And be not conformed to this world: but be ye transformed by the renewing of your mind, that ye may prove what is that good, and acceptable, and perfect, will of God."* Romans 12:1-2. There are three steps in getting your mind renewed, to think like God thinks or to see life from the biblical worldview.

- First you must read the Word of God daily. Again, early in the morning, I read through a one year bible. *"…Give full attention to my word…"* Proverbs 4:20. Don't let anything or anyone come before the Word of God. The devil's strategy is to keep you too busy to give the Word of God your full attention. God's Word is life and it is the key to keeping your mind free and protected.

- Secondly, in renewing your mind, meditate daily in God's Word. *"This book of the law shall not depart out of thy mouth; but thou shalt meditate therein day and night, that thou mayest observe to do according to all that is written therein: for then thou shalt make thy way prosperous, and then thou shalt have good success."* Joshua 1:8. *Meditate* means "to engage in thought or contemplations; to reflect; to digest the Word of God into the soul or mind." By morning, I sit at the feet of Jesus. As I read the Word of God, I reflect on what I read and often write the scripture on an index card. As I meditate, the verse becomes the voice and real faith is born in my heart, and my mind is renewed and protected.

- Thirdly, part of meditation and renewing your mind is the confession of God's Word. Often in the morning, I will give thanks and declare the exchanges of the cross for my full redemption and freedom. He took my sin that I might have His righteousness. He took my selfishness that I might have His unselfishness. He took my fears and worries that I might have His peace. He took my sicknesses that I might have His health. Through the power of God's Word, my mind is being renewed and I maintain my freedom from darkness and demonic intrusion.

4. **A fourth basic step in protecting your mind is the principle of rejection.** You must discipline yourself to guard your mind by rejecting wrong or worldly thoughts. God's thoughts are peaceful and positive. Therefore, refuse and reject negative thoughts such as doubt and unbelief, lust thoughts, condemnation thoughts, bitter thoughts, poor me and pity-party thoughts.

By God's grace, cast down the thoughts of defeat and failure. Joshua and Caleb refused to think like grasshoppers. *"...There are giants in the land, and we are in our own sight as grasshoppers."* Numbers 13:33. Rather, Joshua and Caleb were giant killers, they thought and said, *"...don't fear the people of the land for they are bread for us..."* Numbers 14:9. This is a truth, the first place you lose victory and your freedom to flow in the Holy Spirit is in the mind. If you think poverty, you will not receive our Lord's provision. If you think sickness, you will not receive the healing and health. If you think guilt and stay on a condemnation trip, you will have no sense of righteousness and the boldness of the Lord! The bottom line is that we need to obey and move in the grace of God. II Corinthians 10:4-5, *"The weapons we fight with are not the weapons of the world. On the contrary, they have divine power to demolish strongholds. We demolish arguments and every pretension that sets itself up against the knowledge of God, and we take captive every thought to make it obedient to Christ."* Refuse and reject the negative and bring every thought captive to the obedience of Christ. As you do so, victory and freedom is certain!

5. **The final basic spiritual discipline in freedom from darkness, defeat, and demons is replacement!** *Replace* means "to take the place of; to put something new in place of the old. Replace the old and dark negative thoughts."

In your thinking, replace poverty with God's wealth. It is a promise, *"Bring ye all the tithes into the storehouse, that there may be meat in mine house, and prove me now herewith, saith the LORD of hosts, if I will not open you the windows of heaven, and pour you out a blessing, that there shall not be room enough to receive it. And I will rebuke the devourer for your sakes, and he shall not destroy the fruits of your ground; neither shall your vine cast her fruit before the time in the field, saith the LORD of hosts."* Malachi 4:10-12. Replace guilt with a righteousness mindset. It is a promise, *"For he hath made him to be sin for us, who knew no sin; that we might be made the righteousness of God in him."* II Corinthians 5:21. Replace worry and anxiety with peace. It is a promise, *"...the judgment of our peace was upon him; and with his stripes we are healed."* Isaiah 53:5. Replace unworthiness and selfishness with holiness. It is a promise, *"Wherefore Jesus also, that he might sanctify the people with his own blood, suffered without the gate."* Hebrews 13:12. At the cross He took our selfishness that we might have His unselfishness or holiness. Replace sickness with health and healing. It is a promise, *"Surely, He has borne our sickness and carried away our pains..."* Isaiah 53:4-5. Jesus Christ is our Savior/ Healer.

Let's simply obey Philippians 4:8-9, *"Finally, brethren, whatsoever things are true, whatsoever things are honest, whatsoever things are just, whatsoever things are pure, whatsoever things are lovely, whatsoever things are of good report; if there be any virtue, and if there be any praise, think on these things. Those things, which ye have both learned, and received, and heard, and seen in me, do: and the God of peace shall be with you."*

In closing, I am writing this last chapter of "Deliverance from Darkness, Demons, and Disease" on July 4, 2013, the day we celebrate freedom from the tyranny of an evil English King and his great armies. I believe this to be providence rather than coincidence. May your spirit and mind be filled with His joy and peace all the days of your life in Jesus' name.

Note: The three terms for keeping your mind protected: renewal, rejection, and replacement was gleaned from a teaching by Pastor Mike Ware of Victory Church in Denver, Colorado.

The Good News:

God's plan for your forgiveness of sins and your entrance into Heaven.

1. Every human being is born with a sin nature and all of us sin. *"For all have sinned and fall short of the Glory of God..."* **Romans 3:23**

2. Therefore, all of us are sinners and all of us need a savior. The Good News: *"But God demonstrates His own love toward, in that while we were still sinners, Christ died for us."* **Romans 5:8**

3. Religion, rules, and rituals can't save you from your state of sin and death! Rather, you are invited to have a personal relationship with Jesus Christ. The Good News: *"For the wages of sin is death but the gift of God is eternal life in Christ Jesus our Lord."* **Romans 6:23**

4. Right now…Repent of your sins and turn from your selfishness. Call out to Jesus Christ to be your Lord and Savior. *"…if you confess with your mouth the Lord Jesus and believe in your heart that God raised him from the dead, you will be saved."* **Romans 10:9**

The meaning of being saved: By grace and faith in the redeeming blood of Jesus, a man is delivered from the power of sin, Satan and selfishness into the life of grace, peace and righteousness.

Need Additional Copies?

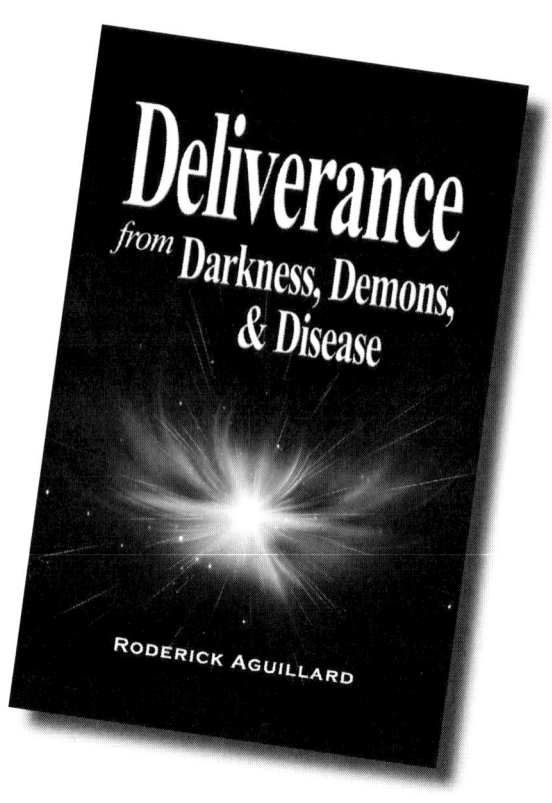

To order more copies of

Deliverance
from Darkness, Demons, & Disease

contact CertaPublishing.com

- ❐ Order online at: CertaPublishing.com/Bookstore
- ❐ Call 855-77-CERTA or
- ❐ Email Info@CertaPublishing.com

Certa
PUBLISHING